DETERMINANTS OF EXECUTIVE COMPENSATION

DETERMINANTS OF EXECUTIVE COMPENSATION

Corporate Ownership, Performance,
Size, and Diversification

ELLEN L. PAVLIK and
AHMED BELKAOUI

QUORUM BOOKS
New York • Westport, Connecticut • London

Library of Congress Cataloging-in-Publication Data

Pavlik, Ellen L.
    Determinants of executive compensation : corporate ownership,
performance, size, and diversification / Ellen L. Pavlik and Ahmed
Belkaoui.
        p.   cm.
    Includes bibliographical references and index.
    ISBN 0-89930-633-0 (alk. paper)
    1. Chief executive officers—Salaries, etc.   2. Executives—
Salaries, etc.   3. Industrial organization.   I. Belkaoui, Ahmed,
1943–   . II. Title.
HD4965.2.P38   1991
658.4′0722—dc20   90-26407

British Library Cataloguing in Publication Data is available.

Library of Congress Catalog Card Number: 90-26407
ISBN: 0-89930-633-0

First published in 1991

Quorum Books, 88 Post Road West, Westport, CT 06881
An imprint of Greenwood Publishing Group, Inc.

Printed in the United States of America

The paper used in this book complies with the
Permanent Paper Standard issued by the National
Information Standards Organization (Z39.48-1984).

10 9 8 7 6 5 4 3 2 1

To our families, here and abroad.

CONTENTS

TABLES AND FIGURES

TABLES

FIGURES

PREFACE

There are various theories about why firms choose the compensation levels and structures they do and what effects these variables are likely to have. Most of the concern has resulted in an effort to ascertain whether executive and managerial compensation levels and changes are related to measures of corporate performance, expressed by either accounting- or market-related measures. To date, the evidence indicates that managerial compensation in general, and CEO compensation in particular, are positively related to a corporation's relative financial position and performance. Although significant, previous research has failed to examine the impact of performance measures on executive compensation in terms of the combined effects of organizational structure and ownership structure. Differences in the internal organizational structure of a firm (based upon differences in diversification strategies) and differences in ownership structure (based upon differences in stock concentration and management stockholdings) are likely to affect the level and structure of executive compensation in general, and CEO compensation in particular. Basically, whether a firm is diversified along a vertical, related, or unrelated strategy, and whether the stock ownership is held by a majority of stockholders or managers will affect the level of compensation for managers. The main thesis of this book is that executive compensation is determined not only by financial performance but also by the type of diversification strategy and ownership structure adopted. This thesis is hypothesized and tested within a path model, which investigates both direct and indirect effects of firm performance, size, ownership structure, and diversification strategy on CEO compensation in a sample of firms from the Fortune 500. The model integrates the concepts and ramifications of: (1) the multidivisional form (m-form) hypothesis, which maintains the superior financial performance of decentralized firms contingent on the choice of appropriate diversification strategy; (2) the ownership structure thesis, which maintains the importance of management control on financial performance; and (3) the compensation thesis, which focuses on the determination of the variables that affect the level and structure of executive compensation in general, and CEO compensation in particular.

The objective of this book is threefold: (1) to review the theory, hypotheses, models, and findings of the m-form hypothesis, the ownership structure hypothesis, and the executive compensation thesis; (2) to construct and test a path analytic model that identifies both the direct and indirect effects of firm performance, size, ownership structure, and diversification strategy on CEO compensation in a sample of firms from the Fortune 500; and (3) to derive policies on the determinants of executive compensation that can be of help to financial analysts, labor unions, investors, members of boards of directors, and researchers interested in the role and ramifications of executive compensation policies.

This book will be of interest to financial analysts, labor unions, investors, members of boards of directors, executives, practicing accountants, academicians, businesspeople, students, social scientists, and others interested in understanding the complex nature and determinants of executive compensation.

THE EXECUTIVE COMPENSATION THESIS

What determines executive compensation? What do compensation-setting boards of directors consider when determining compensation and structuring compensation plans? Early investigations into the area of executive compensation, spurred by economists' interest in firm theory, centered around the question of whether a firm maximizes profits or sales. Out of this came a number of studies on the determinants of executive pay, which included both sales (as a proxy for firm size) and profits (as one measure of firm performance). Currently executive compensation and its relationship to corporate performance have raised issues in managerial, economic, accounting, and financial circles. At issue is the effectiveness of compensation contracts in providing incentives to align manager and shareholder interests, the optimal structuring of compensation packages, the relationship of compensation to corporate performance and shareholder wealth, and the effectiveness of the labor market for executives in determining the level of managerial pay.

As pointed out by Baker, Jensen, and Murphy,

our economic understanding of internal incentive structures which include compensation policies is far from complete. There has been an enormous amount of research in the economics of contracting, but this increasingly technical research has generated few empirical implications, and offers little guidance in understanding actual compensation arrangements.[1]

Among the common features of actual compensation practices are an absence of pay-for-performance systems and overwhelming use of promotion- rather than performance-based incentives. Empirical studies of executive compensation provide some insights and useful information to all concerned with decisions involving executive compensation, although much of the evidence is generally about the relative weights of firm size and performance in determining the amount of CEO pay. In fact, Finkelstein and Hambrick note that "while this stream of research has established important patterns, it has not yielded much explanation for how compensation fits into the total organizational system."[2]

THEORETICAL CONSIDERATIONS

Executive compensation plans lend themselves theoretically to analysis in three different dimensions.[3] First, the functional form of compensation has been explored empirically, setting compensation as the dependent variable in relation to various determinants. Suggested independent variables include size, performance, and proxies for human capital. In this dimension, "the functional form of compensation provides the definition of the relation between pay and performance and the definition of performance."[4]

Second, the composition or relative amount of the components of the compensation package has been analyzed with respect to possible incentive effects. In this type of analysis, compensation becomes an independent variable on which performance is dependent. "The composition of the pay package defines the relative amounts of the components of the package such as cash compensation, fringe benefits, quality of working environment, relationships with co-workers, leisure, etc."[5]

A third dimension of analysis seeks to explore the level of executive compensation, or the total cost of the compensation package to the employer. It is this level that determines the quantity and quality of workers that can be hired by a firm.

While the level of compensation determines who the firm can attract, the functional form determines how the employees perform when hired. The functional form provides the performance incentive for employees; simple increases in the level of compensation will have no effects on effort or performance except the usual income effects of the labor-supply decision.[6]

The Compensation Function

The traditional neoclassical approach to wage determination views performance, often measured by sales and profits, as a principal determinant of executive compensation.[7] The assumption is that sales and/or profits are indicators of executive productivity. More recently two other theoretical views on wage determination have been advanced: the screening hypothesis[8] and the job competition approach.[9]

The screening hypothesis suggests that in a world of imperfect information personal characteristics such as the number of years as CEO (CEO experience) are indicators of qualities conducive to successful performance. The compensation board is likely to take such a variable into account in setting compensation as it will be perceived as an indicator of future performance. The job competition hypothesis favors substantial investment in employee training for a specific job and for the particular conditions of the firm.[10]

The above three theories of wage determination[11] all relate salary to performance, but by joining them together, the implication is that a number of considerations in addition to sales and profits influence compensation. In fact,

decision-making by corporate boards of directors in a world of imperfect information apparently involves extrapolation of historical measures of performance, evaluation of relatively low cost indicators of future performance (age and experience) and determination of necessary premiums to inhibit executive mobility to protect the firm's investment in specific training.[12]

In determining empirically the functional form of compensation, regression equations of the following general form have been employed:

$$R = a + b_1 S + b_2 P + b_3 W + b_4 Z + u$$

Where a is an intercept, the b terms are regression coefficients, u is an error term, and typically

R = a measure of compensation

S = sales

P = profits

W = a measure of shareholder wealth

Z = a vector of either firm-specific or individual-specific characteristics

The relationship of compensation to its determinants would be expected to be concave and the above linear approximation to any segment would include a $>$ 0 as seen below:

COMPENSATION

S,P,W,Z...

In conformity with the above view of the compensation function, Agarwal proposes a conceptual model of executive compensation that comprises both individual and organizational variables.[13] In particular compensation is viewed as a function of job complexity, an employer's ability to pay, and human capital variables. It is expected that since job complexity measures the nature and degree of responsibility of the job itself, it will influence the perception of the value of that job and hence the compensation afforded the individual holding that job. Agarwal reasons that

it (job complexity) is a structural concept relating to what the job is rather than how well it is being performed by the incumbent. As the organizational structure becomes more differentiated functionally, vertically, and spatially, it involves an increasingly complex pattern of interactions and relationships that the executives have to deal with.[14]

With regard to ability to pay, firms with greater ability to pay may maintain higher wage levels in order to increase the quantity and quality of applicants. As Agarwal argues,

the relative shortage of executive talent necessitates that employers pay competitive wages to attract and retain executives. To what extent an employer will in fact be able to do so depends upon his ability to pay. Thus one could argue that, other things being equal, the greater the employer's ability to pay, the higher the level of executive compensation.[15]

The inclusion of human capital variables can be derived from human capital theory,[16] which asserts that the amount of human capital an individual possesses influences productivity, which in turn influences earnings. Thus, "other things being equal, an executive with a greater amount of human capital would be better able to perform his job, and thus be paid more."[17]

Compensation Plans and Agency Theory

The compensation function in a sense defines performance. Compensation plans, then, may be viewed as independent variables on which performance may be measured or depend. In this theoretical framework, incentives may be examined.

Agency theory defines an agency relationship to exist whenever one party (the principal) hires another party (the agent) to perform some service that requires the principal to delegate some decision-making authority to the agent. Agency theory is an appropriate context for examining executive compensation due to the separation of ownership and control in a large firm. Agency theory assumes that all individuals care about financial compensation, wealth, and perquisites, and that managers prefer leisure to hard work. Therefore specification of incentive, monitoring, and bonding relationships that will minimize net costs of the divergence of interests between themselves and the owners is required. The agency model argues that if top executives are compensated only by straight salary, they may not be motivated to take actions that maximize the value of the firm to shareholders. They will overconsume nonpecuniary items such as leisure and other perquisites and not invest sufficient time and effort to increase shareholder wealth. If owners knew of the optimal decisions and actions that should be taken by managers and could observe management's actions, they could direct implementation of such actions. Incentive compensation contracts have been touted as one way to create a commonality of interests between management and owners, but some divergence will always exist due to differences in attitudes toward risk, information asymmetries, and limited or costly monitoring of the actions of management.[18]

Agency theory concentrates on the implications of the separation of ownership and management that exists in the corporate environment. For a single period, the agent's compensation may be defined as a function of performance variables, x and y, denoted $c(x,y)$. An agent will of course attempt to maximize utility subject to some constraint. Holmstrom[19] indicates that $c(x,y)$ is the solution to the following equality:

$$\frac{1}{U'[c(x,y)]} = \lambda + \mu \frac{f_a(x,y|a)}{f(x,y|a)}$$

Where $U(\cdot)$ is the agent's utility function for money—assuming that the principal is risk-neutral

$f(x,y|a)$ is the density function of x and y given the agent's effort

$f_a(x,y|a)$ is the derivative of the density function with respect to the agent's effort

λ is the Lagrange multiplier on the constraint that specifies the lower bound on the level of expected utility that the contract can provide to the agent

$\mu > 0$ is the Lagrange multiplier on the constraint that ensures the agent's choice of effort be incentive-compatible

In addressing the incentive problem, various components are found in compensation plans. Most plans can be characterized as having a fixed salary portion and a variable performance-based portion. Trendwise, a decrease in the fixed portion accompanied by an increase in the variable component is apparent. Compensation plans may also exhibit both short- and long-term (deferred) aspects. The alternative components of compensation as described by Butler and Maher[20] are summarized in Table 1.1.

The rationale offered for the existence of the various components of executive compensation plans is that they reduce the combined tax liability of the firm and its manager, and encourage managers to maximize the value of the firm. Although tax incentives can explain a portion of the popularity of particular components of compensation plans (i.e., stock options), Smith and Watts note that

tax motivations cannot explain the existence of, and variations in, U.S. firms' compensation plans. . . . Further, taxes cannot explain the extent to which bonus plans go to isolate individual performance or why incentive plans are less frequent in regulated

Table 1.1
Components of Compensation

CASH BONUS AND PROFIT SHARING	A periodic, usually annual lump sum cash payment based on corporate performance, merit or job classification. May act as a short term incentive. Comprises 25-40% of total compensation.
STOCK BONUSES	Periodic distribution of shares of stock as an alternative to a cash bonus. Awarded to align interests of managers and shareholders. Usually based on years of service, position or extraordinary performance. Not usually a substantial portion of total compensation.
DEFERRED COMPENSATION	Cash or stock awards in which managers and firms may contribute to purchase stock or defer cash income to future periods. May have long run incentive effects.
STOCK OPTIONS	Rights to purchase stock at a prescribed price within a certain time period.
STOCK APPRECIATION RIGHTS	Rights to increases in stock price from time of award to payment date. Do not involve contribution by manager.
PERFORMANCE SHARES	Contingent stock or unit awards determined by the achievement of a 3-5 year target. Awarded only to senior executives.

industries. On the other hand, the incentive effects of compensation plans can explain these phenomena.[21]

In particular bonus plans and some performance plans explicitly tie compensation to a measure of the firm's value. There is ample historical evidence of compensation contracts that link compensation to reported earnings in order to control managers' expenditures. By the end of the nineteenth century, English bylaws tied management compensation to earnings, and by the early twentieth century earnings-based compensation plans had become the norm in Europe. Similarly by the 1950s, many U.S. compensation schemes included plans tying compensation to earnings.[22] Typically the bonus is tied to ex ante annual accounting profits. This fact may have larger implications for investment and financing decisions of the firm in that "bonus plans give managers incentives to turn down positive net present value (NPV) projects with long pay back and to take negative value projects which impose expenses only after the manager retires."[23]

In order to explore the implications of earnings-based plans in respect to decision making, Narayanan develops a rigorous economic framework to investigate whether making a manager's pay contingent on firm performance tends to make managers "quick profit"-oriented.[24] The development of the model and derivation of the optimal wage policy for the manager is based on the following assumptions: (1) a manager's ability is unknown; (2) a manager's labor is the only factor of production in a competitive labor market; and (3) the output of the firm depends on the ability, nature, and decisions of the manager. In setting compensation, stockholders use output to update their perception of the manager's ability. Narayanan shows "that even when the manager's future wage is based on current and past performance and the stockholders demand short-term profits, the manager does not necessarily make decisions that are short-term profit oriented as long as any information the manager has is common knowledge."[25]

In the case of private information (only managers know their decisions), managers do have an incentive to make decisions that yield short-term results in hopes of enhancing their reputation earlier and increasing their compensation. The model also predicts that more experienced managers or those possessing a longer-term compensation contract will have less incentive to opt for quick return projects, since their ability is more precisely known.

The Level of Executive Compensation: Neoclassical, Tournament, and Social Comparison Models

Conventional neoclassical theory treats managers as any other factor of production, which implies that the most corporations would be willing to pay executives would be an amount equal to the marginal product of their ability, assuming complete labor markets. Furthermore, conventional theory dictates that compensation depends on individual performance. "Many real-world situations, by contrast, offer rewards that depend on an individual's performance relative to others. We call such situations economic contests. . . . Many contests play a useful role as incentive mechanisms."[26] For this reason and because of the existence of large observed discrepancies in levels of compensation afforded CEOs, vice presidents, and lower executives in firms also not explained by conventional theory, it has been suggested that the determination of executive compensation may be viewed as an economic contest or tournament.

Economic contests or tournaments encourage certain types of behavior by offering rewards or prizes. In the case of executive compensation, rewards are indivisible in that there is only one CEO and limited management positions at lower levels. In the case of individualistic rewards, it is argued that incentives are maintained by awarding individual participants in the contest probabilistic chances of winning. The CEO's salary is viewed as the top prize for which competitors "may give up some of the expected salary associated with his or her marginal product, or individual performance. This excess then becomes part of the lottery prize realized as the CEO's salary."[27]

Lazear and Rosen show that when workers are risk-neutral, compensation schemes based on rank in an organization (promotion-based) induce the same efficient allocation of resources as incentive-based compensation schemes.[28]

Also this interpretation suggests that presidents of large corporations do not necessarily earn high wages because they are more productive as presidents but because this particular type of payment structure makes them more productive over their entire working lives. A contest provides the proper incentives for skill acquisition prior to coming into the position.[29]

By viewing executive compensation in the context of a tournament, the likelihood of being rewarded depends on one's performance relative to others. Tournament theory has other implications as well in that it is theorized that tournaments provide lower monitoring costs and risk reduction. On the other hand certain problems are associated with promotion-based tournaments. They may elicit the wrong level of effort from participants or the wrong individuals for the job.

Another possible explanation for what is casually viewed as high compensation amounts for senior executives may come from social comparison theory. In practice, compensation levels are determined by compensation boards consisting of individual decision makers. Social comparison theory suggests that when individuals are sought to serve on these boards, the tendency is to seek those individuals who are marginally better than the CEO on which judgment is to be passed. Furthermore, the theory implies that these boards will anchor their judgments in their own salaries.

While compensation consultants are often used to provide executive salary surveys for the industry, the most immediate comparison set available to the committee members is their own experience. Since this group almost always is comprised of outside directors, it again seems likely that compensation will reflect the average compensation level of the . . . committee.[30]

RESEARCH REVIEW

Determinants of Executive Compensation

Numerous studies have attempted to assess the structural relationship between executive compensation and such determinants as size (sales) and performance, $c = f(x,y)$. Early studies used sales as a proxy for size and profits to measure performance. More recently studies have been characterized by a consideration of broader determinants such as individual and firm characteristics, and the relative importance of different types of performance variables including both accounting- and shareholder-based measures.

Compensation plans approved by boards of directors generally link pay to performance measures that are themselves related to shareholder wealth (such as the accounting profit of the firm). Arguments have been advanced for the inclusion of market measures in addition to accounting measures.[31] Market-based performance measures such as annual stock return have been utilized because such measures impound information about changes in a firm's financial condition which are associated with both current and anticipated actions and events. In addition, the measurement of stock returns is not directly subject to the moral hazard which may underlie financial accounting or other performance measures reported by the executives being evaluated.[32]

Antle and Smith also argue that accounting measures may contain other valuable information for executive performance evaluation purposes in that stock prices impound information relevant for valuing the firm but do not necessarily impound all information relevant for evaluating the performance of the firm's management.[33] Furthermore, "an executive's ability to hedge the systematic or unsystematic risk imposed on him through a compensation plan based on a financial accounting measure is likely to be less than his ability to hedge such risk when the plan is based on a market measure."[34]

These arguments suggest that both accounting- and market-based measures are candidates for consideration in compensation plans linking pay to performance measures.

Theoretical Differences

The sales maximization hypothesis asserts that with increased separation of owners and managers, managers are not necessarily constrained to act in the interest of owners, but rather their own self-interest. The tendency would be to take actions that would increase sales (and size), and sales would be more highly related to compensation than other measures. As a corollary, it has been suggested that there is a differential in compensation for executives of small companies versus large companies.[35]

On the other hand, Lewellen and Huntsman assert that "at the core of most economic analysis of industrial behavior is the proposition that the managers of an enterprise guide its activities in such a way as to maximize the monetary well-being of its owners."[36] This profit maximization hypothesis implies that the amount of compensation afforded managers should be positively and more highly related to profits or performance measures than to sales.

Compensation itself can be defined in different ways. The definition may or may not include bonuses, deferred amounts, nonpecuniary items, and stock-related items (see Table 1.1). Discussions of issues involving the valuation of various components of compensation indicate that salary plus cash bonus is almost always a significant portion of total compensation.[37] In addition, evidence shows that salary plus cash bonus represents between 80 and 90 percent of total compensation.[38] Furthermore, Jensen and Murphy provide evidence that the slope coefficient relating salary plus cash bonus to changes in performance is not statistically different from the slope coefficient that relates total compensation to changes in performance.[39]

Studies on the Determinants of Executive Compensation

Early empirical studies in this area centered on the relationship of sales and/or profits to compensation. One of the first significant studies was made by

McGuire, Chiu, and Elbing. They examined the relationship of executive compensation (as measured by cash plus bonuses) to sales and profits during the period 1953–1959 for forty-five of the one hundred largest U.S. corporations. Their findings indicated a strong positive correlation between sales and executive compensation. Furthermore, "when the boards of directors of an enterprise (or whatever person or persons make such a decision) determines executive compensation, this decision is affected significantly by current or past sales, or by realized changes in sales. . . . Executive compensation is primarily a reward for past sales efforts."[40] Their study was later criticized because it was cross-sectional and only partially measured compensation.

In a study by Lewellen and Huntsman,[41] data on fifty Fortune 500 companies were analyzed for the period 1942–1963. Lewellen utilized multivariate weighted regression analysis and a more comprehensive measurement of compensation in analyzing the relationship of compensation, profits, and sales. He also analyzed the relationship of market value of the firm (as measured by its outstanding stock value), sales, and compensation. Lewellen found (as opposed to McGuire) that reported profits and market values are substantially more important in the determination of executive compensation than sales. Another finding that was rather surprising was that a more comprehensive measure of executive compensation did not perform any better than salary plus bonus. "Specifically, the coefficients of the market value variable have positive signs for all cross-sections no matter which measure of compensation serves as the dependent variable."[42] The critical difference in the two studies seems to be Lewellen's use of weighted regression to correct for collinearity.

Masson, in a study of executive motivations, earnings, and consequent equity performance criticized earlier studies on the basis of their formulation of the compensation function itself. In his opinion, previous studies "omitted a full definition of executive compensation, including present-value aspects of stock options and retirement benefits, and they have excluded executive return from stock ownership as well."[43]

Masson calculates the present value of compensation based on this concept. He then specifies an estimating equation that relates financial return to executives, in the aggregate, to their firm's performance. His aggregation technique is a "zero test." The most striking result is that firms do not pay their executives to maximize sales. Financial incentives of executives do indeed affect stock market performance, and when the financial incentives of executives are aligned with stock market performance, the firm in turn benefits.

In a study of one thousand British companies, Cosh examines the relationship of remuneration of chief executives to company size and profitability.[44] Cosh returns to a less comprehensive measure of compensation. He also considers various theories of executive compensation in order to derive testable implications from them. The neoclassical theory of executive compensation views executives as any other factor of production. Indivisibility of the individual is recognized, and therefore any one individual may have a varying amount of allocative or executive ability. It follows that the individual with the greatest "executive ability" will control the largest firm and hence get the largest amount of compensation. Cosh finds that company size is the major determinant of remuneration to chief executives. Size alone explains on the average 49 percent of the variance in executive pay. By adding profitability as an explanatory variable, 54 percent of the variance is explained. Cosh also notices a difference in what are known as quoted versus nonquoted companies. It appears that for larger companies, size matters more, while for smaller companies, "the results looked quite different. In these groups size alone explained on the average, 19% of the national logarithm of chief executive remuneration, yet the degree of explanation was raised to 34% when profitability was added as a further explanatory variable." [45]

It is interesting to note that Cosh replicates Lewellen and Huntsman's results by using their equation with his data. The equation used by Lewellen and Huntsman has as its dependent variable the ratio of compensation to net assets, which eliminates the effects of scale of operations. By using a log linear form of the equation, Cosh finds size to be a major determinant of compensation.

In their study, Ciscel and Carroll attempt to reconcile the above findings by correcting for problems of multicollinearity, heteroscedasticity, and simultaneous equation bias.[46] The critical difference in their methodology stems from their use of residual profits, defined as profits arising by reducing production costs, which are uncorrelated with sales, in the basic regression equation. Their findings indicate that executives are paid for increasing profits (as measured by accounting data) of the firm whether it be through increased sales or cost reduction. Also since sales is a proxy for the size of a company, decisions concerning compensation are also partly based on this. In Ciscel and Carroll's specification the constant term of the regression is viewed as picking up the equilibrium price of the chief executive officer's time, opportunity cost, or the money payment for general human capital. Ciscel and Carroll conclude that a more robust model is needed, and indicate that "three influences—the market for managerial talent, the external performance of the firm and the internal technical efficiency of production—will be identified for successive years as significant and regular influences on the level of executive compensation." [47]

Hogan and McPheters assert that differences in findings of previous studies are due to data selection.[48] In their study, the emphasis is on the characteristics of the chief executive, so data selection is based on highest compensation, rather than industry (McGuire, Chiu, and Elbing) or sales (Lewellen). Hogan and McPheters add experience, education, and background as independent variables to assess the determinants of compensation. Their findings indicate a strong positive role for sales, a negative role for profits, and a positive role for experience.

Agarwal explains 80 percent of the variance in executive compensation by relating it to job complexity, employer's ability to pay, and human capital variables.[49] Four measures of job complexity—span of control, functional divisions, management levels, and geographic diversity—are utilized. Ability to pay is measured in terms of total profit and rate of return on assets, which have been termed "performance variables" in other studies. The human capital variables consist of educational level, field of study, and work experience.

Hirschey and Pappas explore further the compensation-performance relationship by considering the regulatory and life-cycle influences on managerial incentives.[50] They adopt a log-linear form of the compensation model that includes variables for residual profits and sales. After testing 680 companies in three sectors (industrial, banking, and utilities) they find the following: (1) profit and sales matter for managers of large corporations; (2) in the utility sector, there exists a disincentive to pursue profits, possibly due to regulatory influences, and (3) in the industrial sector, the life-cycle theory of the firm has relevance in that small companies tend to maximize sales, while profits hold more explanatory power in the examination of larger industrial firms.

This is not the case for managers of regulated utilities where substantial and clear incentives for sales maximization are present. This latter finding has important public policy implications as it suggests that, contrary to popular belief, current methods of utility regulation may result in under- rather than overcapitalization.[51]

Murphy contends that past econometric studies, because of their omission of performance-sensitive components, have ignored or diminished to a minor role corporate performance in the determination of executive compensation.[52] His conclusions indicate that firm performance as measured by shareholders' realized return is strongly and positively related to compensation.

This result, which comes as no surprise to economists but may shock editors of many popular business periodicals, is verified in all regressions and seems generally robust to the stock market performance index utilized. Moreover, growth of firm sales—another measure of performance—is also strongly related to executive compensation.[53]

The distinguishing characteristic of Murphy's work is the inclusion of a dummy variable for individual position. His conclusions stress the need to control for firm- and individual-specific variables, rendering some past studies, which omitted these variables, biased and misleading. Lambert and Larker suggest a further refinement—"that cash compensation is more highly associated with differences in accounting returns than with levels of security market returns."[54]

Antle and Smith further extend and define the relationship of accounting profits to compensation by examining the relationship of executive compensation to systematic (industry-wide) and unsystematic changes in profits.[55] Their findings on the importance of relative performance measures are mixed in that

the strongest sample-wide evidence consistent with relative performance evaluation is based on tests which assume only an increasing, not necessarily linear, relation between compensation and the accounting based performance measure. . . . Analogous results involving the market-based performance measure . . . are inconsistent with relative performance evaluation.[56]

The effect of ownership and control in the determination of executive compensation was examined by Gomez-Mejia, Tosi, and Hinkin.[57] They depart from the standard methodology by adding a dummy variable for ownership control (defined as more than 5 percent of the outstanding stock in the hands of an individual or firm not involved in management). Their study demonstrates that "executives in externally controlled firms receive more compensation for performance and less for scale of operation than their counterparts in firms without dominant stockholders."[58]

An interesting twist on the determinants of compensation is offered by Lewellen, Loderer, and Martin, who relate the different components of compensation to firm-specific characteristics.[59] By regressing the cash and current income component on such independent variables as proportion of long-term investment opportunities, age, percentage ownership, and dividend payout and the stock-related proportion of compensation against investment opportunities, age, debt-equity ratios, alphas, and betas, they find a link between the structure of compensation plans and the attributes of firms. More specifically,

the components of senior executive pay are found to vary systematically across firms in a manner that cannot easily be explained by tax effects, and which would indicate that individual elements of pay are aimed at controlling for limited horizon and risk exposure problems. Managerial decisions and the structure of managerial pay therefore appear to be interrelated.[60]

Deckop shows, contrary to earlier studies, that CEOs are not given an incentive to increase firm size through compensation schemes, but rather CEO pay is significantly and positively related to profit as a percentage of sales.[61] By using a longitudinal approach and exploring other determinants such as how a CEO gets a job, he is able to shed more light on the profit-versus-sales controversy. Interestingly, he finds that on the average, CEOs recruited from the outside earn significantly more than internally promoted CEOs, and both earn more than firm founders. In particular, "the difference in compensation was found to be about $100,000. Since this differential in compensation cannot be explained by differences in firm performance (which were held constant), an implication is that job-hopping appears to pay off even at the highest executive level."[62]

More recently, Ely, in a study examining interindustry differences in the relation between executive compensation and firm performance, finds that

the results of the analysis of explicit compensation plans are completely consistent with the expectations for the industry-specific vectors for one of five industries examined. For another two industries the explicit plans provide evidence which, while not directly consistent with these expectations, is not inconsistent with them.[63]

The industry-specific vector of variables used included annual stock return and five income-related accounting variables. Ely's findings also imply that stock measures do not dominate accounting measures as explanatory power for every industry examined.

Gibbons and Murphy also look at industry-specific measures of performance and their relationship to executive compensation for executives from 1,049 corporations from 1974–1986.[64] They examine whether rewarding CEOs based on performance measured relative to aggregate industry or market performance creates incentives to increase shareholder wealth, based on the theoretical argument that "rewarding top-level executives based on performance measured relative to aggregate performance in the industry or market creates incentives to take actions increasing shareholder wealth while insuring executives against the vagaries of the stock and product markets that are beyond their control."[65] Their results suggest that CEO compensation is more strongly related to performance relative to aggregate market movements than industry movements.

By analyzing the variance in compensation for 439 large firms for the period 1981–1985 in terms of company, occupation, hierarchical position, human capital, and sales variables, Leonard finds that "position in the corporate hierarchy is one of the strongest determinants of pay."[66] Although individual company differences account for 8 percent of the variance in pay, position in the corporate hierarchy accounts for an even greater 10 percent of the variance. In his sample executives in flat organizations (those with only one level of subordinates) received as much as 32 percent less compensation than their counterparts in organizations more hierarchically structured (those having five subordinate levels).

Abowd, in an attempt to measure more clearly the degree of performance sensitivity in compensation systems, develops a framework that allows for analysis of the effects of interactions between current performance and current compensation on subsequent performance.[67] Performance is measured in terms of two accounting-based measures of firm performance: a measure of economic performance of the firm and a market measure of firm performance. His findings indicate that firms that tie compensation to either economic performance or market measures of performance experience better performance on that particular measure in the future, while accounting performance measures are weakly associated with changes in executive compensation.

In a recent study, Belkaoui hypothesizes that corporate boards control managerial behavior by making compensation decisions related not only to performance and size of firm, but also on the basis of organizational effectiveness and social performance.[68] Organizational effectiveness is measured as the combined score obtained from survey results for the following attributes: quality of management, quality of products/service, innovativeness, value as a long-term investment, soundness of financial position, ability to attract, develop, and keep talented people, responsibility to community and environment, and wise use of assets. Social performance is measured in terms of responsibility to community and environment. Findings indicate that in addition to previously tested determinants, executive compensation is positively associated with external perceptions of industry analysts and executives, regarding organizational effectiveness.

Summary and Implications

Studies related to the determination of the functional form of executive compensation are summarized in Table 1.2. The evidence examined appears to indicate that compensation will vary with size, performance, industry, type of control, and specific characteristics of the individuals and firms involved. It should be noted that the results of studies may differ due to the measure of compensation used, the method of data selection, and the methodology involved. Since compensation contracts themselves are very complicated, measurements using only direct pay may not be sufficient for analysis. Some important properties of CEO compensation make data difficult to use in empirical research. Some factors that may easily blur or distort empirical results include: (1) the receipt by the CEO of nonfinancial rewards; and (2) the many forms of compensation packages, which often include salary, bonus, benefits stock options, premium contributions, deferred income, and long-term contingent compensation. ·

The recent inclusion of industry-specific variables, human capital variables, and control variables seems to have added to the body of knowledge on the determinants of compensation, but further refinement is needed. In the case of human capital factors, Finkelstein and Hambrick argue that "in the absence of concrete measures of a CEO's marginal product, his or her credentials may be relied upon to estimate worth. Particularly promising is the possibility that a high value is attached to a person whose attributes match the firm's particular needs."[69]

Incentive Effects of Compensation Contracts

Studies suggest that the incentive effects of compensation contracts are important properties of CEO compensation make data difficult to use in empirical research. Some factors that may easily blur or distort empirical results include: (1) the receipt by the CEO of nonfinancial rewards; and (2) the many forms of effects of various types of contracts on acquisition decisions. In this context compensation becomes the independent variable on which performance depends.

Effect of Adoption of Plans on Shareholder Wealth

Masson finds that firms use stock market return as a determinant of executive compensation and in turn that this element may be the most important determinant in changes in executive compensation.[70] This implies that the structure of the compensation contract influences or provides incentives for management

Table 1.2
Determinants of Executive Compensation

STUDY	COMPENSATION MEASURE	INDEPENDENT VARIABLES	SAMPLE	METHODOLOGY	FINDINGS
McGuire Chiu Elbing (1962)	Cash salary plus bonus	Sales Profits	45 Large cos. 1953-1959	Correlation Analysis	Strong correlation between Sales & Compensation
Lewellen Huntsman (1970)	Cash salary plus bonus plus the sum of all current income equiva- lents	Sales Profits Market Value of stock	50 Large Manufacturers (1942-1963)	Weighted Regression	Profits & equity market values are more important than sales/the measure of of compensation did not matter
Masson (1971)	After-tax present value of current and promised future returns	Sales EPS Net Worth	3 industries 3-5 top executives 39 companies (1947-1966)	Zero-test Aggregation	Firms do have stock market return as a determinant of compensation. Firms do not pay for sales maximization.

Study	Dependent Variable	Independent Variable	Sample	Method	Findings
Cosh (1975)	After-tax salary, bonus and estimated money value of benefits in kind	Rate of return on Assets Net Assets	1600 U.K. Cos. (1969-1971)	Log linear form of regression	Company size is major determinant. Differences found in quoted vs. non-quoted companies. Inter-industry differences.
Ciscel Carroll (1980)	Cash salary plus bonus	Residual Profit Sales	230 large industrials (1970-1971) and (1973-1976)	Regression	Mixed determinants include sales growth, cost control and profits.
Hogan McPheters (1980)	Salary, bonus and contractually obligated deferred compensation	Sales Profits Vector of personal & human capital characteristics	45 executives (1975)	Ordinary Least Squares	Sales positively related Profits negatively related. Age variable is significant. Negative for years of service. Positive for years as CEO.
Hirschey Pappas (1981)	Total remuneration/Salary plus bonus plus deferred amounts	Net Income after tax Total Revenues	680 large firms Industrials, Banks and Utilities (1977)	Log Linear Regression	Dual profit and sales incentives exist in industrials. In utility sector there exists disincentives toward profit maximization.

Table 1.2 (Continued)

STUDY	COMPENSATION MEASURE	INDEPENDENT VARIABLES	SAMPLE	METHODOLOGY	FINDINGS
Agarwal (1981)	Salary plus Bonus	Job complexity Employer's ability to pay Human Capital	168 life insurance company executives	Multiple Regression	Job complexity and employer's ability to pay more significant than human capital
Murphy (1985)	Salary, Bonus deferred amounts stock options (Before taxes)	Sales, Stock index Stock variance Dummy variable for position	500 executives from 73 U.S. manufacturers (1964-1981)	Time Series	Performance as measured by shareholder return strongly related to compensation. Important to control for individual and firm differences.
Antle Smith (1986)	After tax current income equivalent	ROA Return on common stock	39 firms- 3 industries (1947-1977)	Time Series Regression	Mixed on whether relative performance measures are are important
Lambert Larker (1987)	Cash compensation	ROE Security market returns	370 firms (1970-1984)	Time Series Multiple Regression	Cash compensation more positively associated with differences in accounting returns

Study	Compensation Measure	Variables	Sample	Method	Findings
Gomez-Mejia Tosi Hinkin (1987)	Salary plus current bonus and long term income	Scale (multiple indices) Performance (multiple indices) Dummy variable for owner vs. manager control	71 large manufacturing (1979-1982)	Regression	Performance is significant for owner controlled firms, while scale is more significant for manager controlled firms
Lewellen Loderer Martin (1987)	Salary plus bonus and after-tax related compensation	Proportion of firm's investment opportunities that are long term, age, stock ownership, Dividend payout, Debt/Equity ratio	5 highest paid executives in 49 large manufacturing firms (1964-1973)	Regression	Found support for mix of compensation components and attributes of firms
Ely (1988)	Net after tax sum of cash, bonuses, stock and performance related elements	Average total assets Firm performance	237 firms in 5 industries	Regression	Compensation is (1988) positively related to industry specific vectors of performance variables

Table 1.2 (Continued)

STUDY	COMPENSATION MEASURE	INDEPENDENT VARIABLES	SAMPLE	METHODOLOGY	FINDINGS
Deckop (1988)	Salary plus Bonus	Profit as a % Sales, Sales, How CEO obtained position, human capital	CEO's of 120 firms in 12 industries	Pooled cross section time series model	Compensation positively related to profit as a % Sales. No incentive to increase firm size. Compensation differed depending on how CEO obtained job.
Belkaoui (1990)	Salary plus Bonus and Salary, bonus and long-term compensation	Net income, Organizational Effectiveness, Social Performance, and Sales	155 firms from 28 industries- 1986	Regression	Compensation positively related to profit, organizational effectiveness, and sales. Negatively related to social performance
Leonard (1990)	Salary plus Bonus	Company, Occupation, Hierarchical Position, Human capital, Sales, Return on equity	Managers from 439 firms (1981- 1985)	Regression	Pay is strongly hierarchically determined. Accounting measures of performance not significantly related to level of executive pay

Study	Compensation	Performance Measures	Sample	Method	Findings
Abowd (1990)	Salary plus Bonus	Return on assets, Return on equity, After-tax gross economic return, Shareholder return	Managers at 250 large corporations (1981-1986)	Regression	Accounting based measures of performance weakly associated with compensation, stronger evidence for economic and market measures
Gibbons Murphy (1990)	Salary plus Bonus	Return on common stock, Industry return	1,668 executives from 1,049 firms (1974-1986)	Regression	CEO compensation increases are positively related to firm's relative financial performance

decisions. "A structure of executive financial returns which emphasizes the stock market return of the firm should have two benefits. First, the executives of the firm should be working in the interests of the owners of the firm, the stockholders. Second, the executives should be emphasizing the present value of profits of the firm." [71]

In a study examining one aspect of the incentives question, Larker states that "the hypothesis that corporate compensation schemes affect corporate decision-making is an important conceptual linkage in the incentive arguments which are now common in accounting and economic research." [72] He finds evidence supporting the existence of incentive effects by comparing the adoption of a performance plan (long-term) compensation scheme and its effects on capital expenditures and security prices, as compared to companies not having comparable plans. His results indicate, relative to similar control firms, that the adopting firms experienced significant increases in capital investment and positive security market reactions.

Brickley, Bhagat, and Lease attempt to assess the relationship of various types of long-term compensation contracts on shareholder wealth. [73] Although no one type of long-range plan increased shareholder wealth more than others, all were met with positive stock market reactions. The implication is that different types of plans may be appropriate in different circumstances.

In a study of incentives behind the adoption of stock option plans for executives, Long attempts to identify the reasons for adoption of these types of plans. He maintains that if "the plans were intended to provide appropriate managerial incentives that could not be provided any other way, then they would have been adopted and used irrespective of their tax treatment." [74] Long's evidence supports both motivations for adoption, but is stronger for the tax minimization argument.

As in prior studies, Tehranian and Waegelein also find positive stock market reaction to announcements of short-term compensation plans by firms. [75] Waegelein extends this analysis of the adoption of short-term bonus plans by studying effects of corporate expenditures. [76] He confirms the positive stock market reaction and also finds significant relative increases in capital expenditures associated with the adoption of such plans. He also tests for advertising and research and development, for which the results are not significant. Summarizing, "the results of this study provide evidence that the introduction of a short-term compensation scheme is associated with changes in the decisions of managers. Specifically, companies adopting bonus plans showed significant relative increases in capital expenditures." [77]

Incentive effects have also been found to exist in executive termination contracts. Lambert and Larker examined the relationship of the adoption of "golden parachutes" and security market reactions, finding "that Golden Parachute adoption is associated with a statistically significant and positive security market reaction. This is consistent with the hypothesis that Golden Parachutes have a favorable effect on the actions of top executives." [78]

In a recently published study, Kahn and Sherer depart from previous work on the issue of pay for performance by using subjective data on managerial performance and examining the impact of bonus pay on subsequent managerial performance.[79] Previous studies on the effect of the adoption of incentive plans indicate a link to firm performance measured in terms of increased shareholder wealth. Kahn and Sherer argue that "it is not clear, however, whether there are actual incentive effects or, on the contrary, the adoption of executive bonus plans is proposed by managers only when they expect to benefit from such schemes."[80] Their findings indicate that bonus plans for managers in high-level positions, at corporate headquarters, with low seniority are more sensitive to managerial performance, and managers in this category have higher subsequent performance ratings.

Table 1.3 summarizes studies on the components of compensation plans and related incentive effects. The empirical evidence indicates that executive compensation plans do provide incentives to minimize agency costs by better aligning manager decisions with stockholder interests. The type of plan and the relative weights of given components of the plan appear to play a role in influencing decisions. Further studies are needed to distinguish between the effects of alignment of manager and stockholder interests, managers' maximization of their future income, and minimization of the tax liability of the executive and the firm.

Compensation Plans as Determinants of Accounting Principle Decisions

One area of concentration in empirical research has been the effect of compensation plans on management's choice among generally accepted accounting principles. This stream of research has concentrated on bonus plans rather than performance plans. Bonus plans are such that a bonus is awarded in most years, and if awarded, the maximum amount is a positive linear function of reported accounting earnings. The assumption herein is that compensation increases under a bonus arrangement as accounting earnings increase. This has led to the frequently tested bonus plan hypothesis: "Ceteris paribus, managers of firms with bonus plans are more likely to choose accounting procedures that shift reported earnings from future periods to the current period."[81]

Bowen, Noreen, and Lacey hypothesize "that, ceteris paribus, firms with management compensation packages explicitly tied to reported earnings will have a greater propensity to capitalize interest than firms that do not have such plans."[82] Their study indicates that this hypothesis should be rejected.

Healy suggests differently.[83] He includes the fact that bonus plans are a piecewise linear function with lower and often upper bounds. This fact contradicts the previous proposition that managers will always choose income-increasing discretionary accounting policies in light of bonus schemes tied to profits. Rather, "managers are more likely to choose income-decreasing accruals when their bonus plan upper and lower bounds are binding, and income-

Table 1.3
Incentive Effects of Compensation Plans

AFFECT OF THE ADOPTION OF DIFFERENT TYPES OF PLANS ON SHAREHOLDER WEALTH

STUDY	SUBJECT	METHODOLOGY	RESULTS AND COMMENTS
Masson (1971)	Investigated performance of firms with different emphasis on various components	Estimated equation relating performance to proportion of compensation tied to sales, stock performance and profits	Firms with plans that emphasize maximization of stock market return outperform those that emphasize other performance variables. Small, non-random sample.
Larker (1983) _Larcker_	Effect of adoption of performance plans on capital expenditures and market reaction	Compared 25 adopting firms with control firms. Computation of capital investment growth rates 6 years prior and 2 years after	Adoption of a performance plan is associated with an increase in corporate investment and a favorable stock market reaction
Brickley Bhagat Lease (1985)	Effect of changes in long term components	175 plans studied in event-time analysis. Individual components analyzed.	Long range plans are met with positive stock market reaction, although no one type of plan increased shareholder wealth more than others
Long (1988)	Incentives behind adoption of stock option plans	Reviews evolution of stock option plans and parallel tax treatment to ascertain role of incentives and taxes	Evidence supports both incentive and tax motives. Appears stronger for tax motive.

24

Table 1.3 (Continued)

STUDY	SUBJECT	METHODOLOGY	RESULTS AND COMMENTS
Tehranian Waegelein (1985)	Stock price reaction to introduction of short term plans	Average abnormal returns are estimated	Announcement of short term plan adoption is associated with positive abnormal returns. Consistent with Larker's 1983 findings on long term plans.
Waegelein (1988)	Short term plans and their effect on expenditures	139 matched pairs of firms analyzed with respect to differentials in advertising, R & D, and capital expenditures	Adoption of short term bonus plans associated with an increase in capital expenditures only. Also positive stock market reaction.
Lambert Larker (1985)	Stock price reaction to termination agreements	Cross-sectional regression of standardized security market reactions and variables related to Golden Parachute termination agreements	Adoption of a golden parachute plan is associated with statistically significant positive security market reaction
Kahn Sherer (1990)	Examination of relationship of financial incentives and performance using subjective measures of manager performance	Analyzed personnel data on 92 middle to upper level managers of one firm 1984-1985	Managers for whom bonuses are more sensitive to performance have higher subsequent performance

increasing accruals when their bonus plan bounds are not binding."[84] Healy's findings indicate that bonus schemes do in fact create incentive effects for managers to maximize the value of their bonus awards. In a recent study, Mc-Nichols and Wilson tested a more general hypothesis, motivated by Healy on earnings management, and developed a new proxy for discretionary accruals.[85] Their findings support the hypothesis that firms "manage their earnings by choosing income-decreasing accruals when income is extreme."[86]

Two additional studies, Healy, Kang, and Palepu[87] and Abdel-Khalik, Chiu, and Ghicas,[88] examine the effect of accounting procedure changes on executive compensation. Healy et al. attempt to determine whether, after accounting procedures have been changed, salary and bonus are based on reported earnings or earnings under the original accounting method. The "results indicate that (1) subsequent to these changes salary and bonus payments are based on reported earnings, rather than earnings under the original accounting method, and (2) the potential compensation effect of the change is small compared to the effect of economy- or industry-wide changes in compensation."[89] Abdel-Khalik et al. obtain results that indicate that "top executives' compensation changes with the real (instead of income) consequences of accounting changes."[90]

Table 1.4 summarizes studies on the effect of compensation plans on accounting principle choice and the bonus plan hypothesis.

Compensation Plans and Acquisition Decisions

The incentive question has also been examined by Lewellen, Loderer, and Rosenfeld in light of acquisition decisions and the percentage of stock ownership of managers.[91] They find a consistently positive relationship between stock returns from mergers and percentage ownership of stock held by senior managers, concluding that "high costs to management lessen the likelihood that shareholder wealth will be sacrificed in mergers for the sake of personal gains by the acquiring firm's managers."[92] Lambert and Larker extend this work by examining whether managers selecting acquisitions that decrease shareholder wealth obtain any benefits as a result of the acquisition.[93] They find a small increase in cash compensation, which is more than offset by a decline in the value of their stockholdings.

Incentive effects of long-term "performance plans" are again analyzed by Tehranian, Travlos, and Waegelein in light of corporate acquisition decisions.[94] They look at the effect of differential horizons in compensation contracts and merger decisions consistent with owners' interest. After controlling for managers' stock ownership, their findings indicate "that bidding firms that compensate their executives with long-term performance plans experience a significantly favorable stock market reaction around the announcements of acquisition proposals, while bidding firms without such plans experience a significant unfavorable stock market reaction at the announcement of their acquisition proposals."[95] The above implies that performance plans might be an effective mechanism to align the interest of stockholders and managers. As far as incen-

Table 1.4

Effects of Compensation Plans on Accounting Principle Decisions

STUDY	DESCRIPTION	FINDINGS
Bowen Noreen Lacey (1981)	Used univariate and multivariate tests to examine decision to capitalize interest.	Firms with explicit management compensation agreements tied to earnings are no more likely to capitalize interest than those without.
Healy (1985)	Examined impact of bonus plans on accrual decisions. Model includes the fact that bonus plans are piecewise linear functions with lower and often upper bounds, instead of treating the plan as a dummy variable.	Bonus plans create incentives to select accounting procedures that maximize their bonus. Managers select income increasing accruals when upper or lower bounds of plan are not binding. Income decreasing accruals are more likely chosen when the lower or upper bounds are binding.
McNichols Wilson (1988)	Examines evidence of earnings management and tests the hypothesis that firms with extreme earnings will choose income-decreasing accruals.	By introducing a new proxy for discretionary accruals, they find evidence that firms manage earnings by choosing income decreasing accruals when income is extreme.
Healy Kang Palepu (1987)	Examined how compensation changes after an accounting change	Subsequent to accounting changes, salary and bonus are based on reported earnings and the compensation effect is small compared to economy or industry wide changes in compensation
Abdel-Khalik Chiu Ghicas (1987)	Effect of accounting methods on compensation Tested Bonus hypothesis and hypothesis of rationality of compensation schemes	Found support for hypothesis of rationality of compensation schemes

tive effects, they also find evidence of a larger increase in postacquisition earnings per share of firms having long-term performance plans as compared to those without.

Studies of the incentive effects of compensation plans and acquisition decisions are summarized in Table 1.5.

The Level of Compensation and Effectiveness of the Labor Market for Executives

The level of executive compensation has been defined theoretically as the efficient wage determined by the operation of a rational labor market for ser-

Table 1.5
Compensation Plans and Acquisition Decisions

STUDY	DESCRIPTION	FINDINGS
Lewellen Loderer Rosenfeld (1985)	Studied relationship of abnormal stock returns and % of stock ownership	Consistent positive and often significant relationship between abnormal stock returns from merger and % of acquiring company's common stock held by senior management
Lambert Larker (1987)	Studied effect on compensation and wealth associated with acquisitions that decrease shareholder wealth	Total compensation and wealth effect is negative and significant for decisions that decrease shareholder wealth
Tehranian Travlos Waegelein (1987)	Effect of long term performance plans on shareholder wealth in acquisition decisions	Bidding firms with long term plans experience significant favorable stock market reaction at the time of of the acquisition announcement

vices (i.e., decision making) provided by executives.[96] If this theory is correct, executives who perform well in their decision making would be rewarded well, while those who do not perform well would somehow be sanctioned. Casual observation suggests an area for investigation: Does the labor market for executives effectively deal with executives who make decisions that adversely affect performance and shareholders? Several studies have presented empirical evidence on this point and will be reviewed here. A second empirical reality concerning the level of managers' salaries is the presence of large differences between CEO salaries and those executives only "one breath away."

Theoretical Considerations

Some empirical observations related to compensation levels and effectiveness of the labor market in aligning manager and shareholder interest cannot be totally explained in the context of neoclassical labor market theory. If CEO pay is viewed as a labor market response, then it should depend on supply and demand. The labor market for executives sets a minimum amount and range of compensation, but is it efficient in doing so?

Finkelstein and Hambrick argue that "the labor market for top managers is relatively inefficient, leading generally to an upward bias in CEO pay."[97] Inefficiencies arise on the supply side due to ambiguity of the talent of CEOs and amorphous boundaries. On the demand side, they argue that often the number of openings is artificially restricted due to the reluctance of firms to go "outside" for a new CEO. The above inefficiencies along with the potential role of compensation consultants in the determination of the level of executive compensation may introduce this observed upward bias in compensation levels. "Even granting the possibility of labor market inefficiencies, the theory of marginal product should still apply for CEOs. However, managerial contributions are elusive. Managerial work is known for its ambiguity and lack of clear cause and effect."[98] For this reason, the theory of tournaments and social comparison theory have been tested empirically for their possible contribution to this area.

Studies Examining the Level
of Compensation and Labor Market Efficiency

Benston tests a form of the self-serving managerial hypothesis: "Managers of conglomerates are hypothesized to effect firm-enlarging actions that yield greater remuneration for them but losses for shareholders,"[99] which implies that managers act in their own self-interest as opposed to that of shareholders. By examining personal financial gains and losses achieved by managers engaged in extensive merger activities and comparing these to gains and losses in shareholder wealth, Benston finds no support for this hypothesis. Benston also finds a generally positive relationship between officers and directors leaving their firms and poor stock market performance. Although it would be speculative, the reason behind the departure of certain executives may be anticipation of possibly losing their positions due to decisions that adversely affected shareholder wealth.

A consistent result was observed by Coughlin and Schmidt, along with evidence of the existence of a rational labor market, that is one that disciplines managers for inappropriate decisions.[100] Their findings indicate that terminations are more likely to occur after decreases in shareholder wealth.

Kerr and Bettis reexamine the results of Benston and Coughlin and Schmidt and ask again, "Do Boards of Directors forsake their obligation to shareholders by failing to use compensation as a control mechanism?"[101] They criticize past studies for lack of consistency in defining stock performance and lack of an adjustment to salary data to account for a one-year lag in salary payout. The results obtained by Kerr and Bettis suggest, contrary to previous studies, "that, in general boards of directors do not consider performance of a firm's stock when changing CEOs' salaries and bonuses. Neither overall market movements nor abnormal returns were associated with adjustments in compensation. . . . At worst, results suggest that boards ignore their responsibility to shareholders."[102]

Johnson et al. focus on changes in shareholder wealth at the time of an unexpected death of a CEO in order to gain insights as to the market for executives.[103] Specifically, "the incumbent manager's death enables shareholders to hire a replacement manager without incurring the costs of dismissing or recontracting with the former manager. Such conditions should produce a positive common stock price reaction to the unexpected death of the incumbent manager."[104] There are negative security market reactions to the death of a CEO who was not a founder. This appears to imply that certain executives are not "overpaid" relative to their contributions to shareholder wealth when compared to potential replacements.

Lambert and Larker also explore the effects of large corporate acquisitions on executive compensation levels.[105] If it is true that size (sales) is a determinant of executive compensation, as some earlier studies suggest, the easiest way for an executive to increase compensation would be through acquisiton decisions. In their study, they examine the effects of corporate acquisitions on compensation and wealth of top executives that make infrequent acquisition decisions. In the case of acquisitions that adversely affect shareholder wealth (as measured by negative security market reaction) executives experienced a small increase in cash compensation, which was more than offset by a decrease in wealth as measured by their stockholdings. In the case of acquisitions that increased shareholder wealth, executives experienced increases in both cash compensation and wealth. Their study provides evidence on both incentives and support for the operation of the labor market as theoretically described.

Another interesting question examined by Salancik and Pfeffer is whether an executive has the ability to influence tenure decisions.[106] Their evidence suggests a direct relationship between stock ownership and tenure. The existence of this relationship tends to deemphasize the relationship of tenure to firm performance. Their study indicates that in management-controlled firms (firms in which no one individual or group owns greater than 4 percent of the outstanding stock), capital markets impose a discipline on managers in that tenure varies directly with performance. Furthermore, evidence of this positive relationship does not exist in the case of owner-controlled firms (firms in which the CEO owns greater than 4 percent of the outstanding stock).

Most recently, O'Reilly, Main, and Crystal examined factors that may influence the setting of compensation levels in light of two models: the tournament model and the social comparison model.[107] In the tournament model, the top CEO's compensation is viewed as a prize in a lottery for which lower managers give up a portion of their current compensation to participate. Their particular test of tournament theory in this context was without support.

However, their test of the social comparison theory provides evidence that compensation levels are positively related to compensation levels of the members of the compensation-setting board. Social comparison theory, a social-psychological explanation of compensation, asserts that individuals have a need to evaluate their opinions and abilities, and in doing so will choose as a standard other individuals who are perceived to have similar opinions and abilities. When making comparisons individuals tend to select others who are slightly better. The implication for members of compensation-setting boards is that they will anchor their judgments in their own salaries, or the salaries of other CEOs perceived as similar or slightly better. In light of the findings of O'Reilly, Main, and Crystal, social comparison theory represents a potential future research area that may provide additional insights into compensation decisions.

With regards to tournament theory, Ehrenberg and Bognanno suggest that empirical results obtained by analyzing data on professional golf tournaments may be relevant for the design of compensation systems of corporate executives.[108] Their evidence suggests that the level and structure of prizes in PGA tournaments influence players' performance. Furthermore, they assert that "although studies of sports tournaments are of interest in themselves, there is the broader question of the extent to which tournament theory can help to provide an explanation for the structure of compensation we observe among corporate executives."[109] In the world of corporate executives it is implied that tournament-type pay structures may elicit desired performance under certain conditions.

Summary and Implications

Studies in this area are summarized in Table 1.6. Evidence supports the existence of a rational labor market for executives that provides discipline on certain decisions of certain managers, thus reducing agency costs by providing incentives. The literature also suggests that a company's shareholder wealth is dependent on the continued employment of an incumbent manager. Wealth effects occur because the manager possibly possesses some firm specific human capital. The implication is that future studies of compensation need to explore the possible explanatory power of this human capital aspect and its link to the level of executive compensation. It also appears from casual observation of actual levels of executive compensation that there is a need to refine current marginal product analysis theory of the determination of the level of executive compensation.

There is also a need to further examine whether external markets in fact operate efficiently as a control on the CEO's actions. Furthermore the internal control devices available to boards of directors, which include termination and incentive plans, are deserving of future attention.

The functional form of compensation has been tested empirically in order to ascertain the determinants of compensation. Likely candidates include size, accounting-based performance variables, stock market-based measures, industry-specific variables, and individual characteristics. In light of mixed empirical results on the relative importance of size versus performance, there is a need for research directed toward the broader determinants of executive compensation—personal characteristics of individual executives:

The significant influence of experience upon compensation levels is shown by the importance of the age variable. The indirect evidence drawn from the variable measuring years as chief executive suggests that specific "on-the-job" training as a chief executive commands a wage premium, independent of performance; but mobility at the lower ranks also has a positive effect.[110]

The nature of control present in a firm also needs to be explored:

Currently, executive compensation is attracting extensive critical comment—not surprising, since over the past ten years the salaries and bonuses of CEOs have increased about

Table 1.6
Level of Compensation and Labor Market Efficiency

STUDY	SUBJECT	METHODOLOGY	RESULTS & COMMENTS
Benston (1985)	Do executives lose more than monetary wealth (their jobs) as a consequence of poor performance?	Comparison of geometric average share price returns of the year an officer leaves and 2 previous years	Findings indicate a generally positive relationship between executives leaving their firms and poor stock performance.
Coughlin Schmidt (1985)	Are management changes along with compensation changes methods utilized to control top management?	Tested whether frequency of CEO turn-over is related to past stock performance	Regression results indicate stock price performance and the probability of a change in CEO are inversely related
Kerr Bettis (1987)	Do boards of directors reward executives on the basis of financial returns to shareholders?	Analyzed data on compensation and stock reaction in 129 cases using time event methodology for years 1977 and 1980.	Suggest that neither variation in abnormal returns nor overall market movements influence compensation to top executives.
Johnson McGee Nagarajan Newman (1985)	Wealth effects of sudden CEO death	Examined stock response to death	Stock market reaction is positive in some cases (founders) and negative in others
Salancik Pfeffer (1980)	Relationship of tenure, performance and control	Examined 32 firms of two classes—owner and manager controlled with respect to size and performance	Executive retention is correlated with stock price share appreciation for management controlled firms

Table 1.6 (Continued)

STUDY	SUBJECT	METHODOLOGY	RESULTS AND COMMENTS
O'Reilly Main Crystal (1988)	Factors affecting setting of compensation	Using data from 105 firms tested 3 hypotheses: 1. Compensation varies with size and performance, 2. The larger the # of V.P.s the greater the difference in compensation levels and 3. CEO's compensation is positively related to salaries of compensation board members	Found weak associations between compensation and size, profit, a negative relationship for # of V.P.s, and a strong positive association for third hypothesis.
Ehrenberg Bognanno (1990)	Incentive effects of tournaments in the design of compensation systems for CEOs	Using data from 1987 European PGA golf tournament, tested whether the level and structure of rewards are influenced by player's performance	Found that the level and structure of rewards are influenced by performance and tournament theory may have relevance in setting level and structure of CEO pay

40 percent faster than the average hourly earnings for nonfarm workers. CEOs' ability to influence their own pay levels, subject to a few constraints, may in part explain this trend.[111]

The type of ownership structure present in a firm significantly affects CEO pay. In owner-controlled firms, managers appear to be in a riskier position, and are primarily rewarded on the basis of performance, while in manager-controlled firms compensation is more significantly related to firm size, which is a more stable factor. The consideration of ownership structure appears to provide an explanation for the inconclusiveness of past empirical work on the relative importance of size versus performance.

Furthermore, Salancik and Pfeffer suggest that power or control, defined in terms of stock ownership, plays a role in mediating the relationship of firm performance and executive tenure.[112] Common sense dictates that when a firm is performing poorly, replacement of the manager is expected. However, it has been argued that if managers have significant control of firms in the form of stockholdings, they are insulated from opposition and the relationship of performance and tenure is said to be mediated by ownership. A similar rationale that also needs to be explored applies to executive compensation decisions. The ownership structure of a firm may play a role in mediating the relationship of firm performance and executive compensation decisions.

With few exceptions, previous research has not examined CEO compensation in multiple industries and labor markets. Such research would involve comparison of factors like barriers to entry (affecting demand for CEOs in a particular industry), industry growth, industry volatility (turnover of CEOs), and compensation levels.[113]

Another possible factor deserving future consideration because of its potential role in the determination of executive compensation is the internal control mechanisms within the firm. It has been argued that forces outside the firm impose a discipline on poor managers in the form of corporate mergers, acquisitions, and takeovers, which are beneficial to shareholders. Coughlin and Schmidt argue that firms have internal control mechanisms such as compensation changes and management changes available to impose discipline on managers.[114] The central question here is if they use these devices. Compensation boards do control managers' behavior through compensation decisions and management termination decisions related to firm stock price performance, a measure of shareholder wealth. Future research should be directed at investigating the consideration of internal corporate control mechanisms in the determination of executive compensation.

In a recently published study, Tosi and Gomez-Mejia examine "the extent to which monitoring and incentive alignment of CEO compensation and influence patterns of various actors on CEO pay vary as a function of ownership distribution within the firm."[115] Their findings, based on reports of 175 chief compensation officers, support the contention that the level of monitoring and incentive alignment devices utilized in the determination of CEO pay differ with respect to the ownership structure of the firm. Specifically, in owner-controlled firms (those in which a single individual or institution outside the firm owns 5 percent or more of the company's stock) the level of monitoring and incentive alignment is greater than in manager-controlled firms (those in which no single individual or group outside the firm owns 5 percent or more of the company's stock).

Current economic models suggest that an increase in firm performance requires greater effort (resulting in disutility) on the part of the manager or executive. To increase expected utility of the individual, incentives in the form of monetary rewards linking pay to performance should be observed. Empirical evidence, however, suggests that performance-based bonuses seldom account for an important part of a worker's compensation.[116] There is a need for an

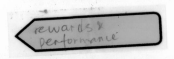
rewards &
performance

economic explanation of actual compensation practices such as the absence of pay-for-performance incentives, the overwhelming use of promotion-based incentive plans, the role of profit-sharing plans, and the biased and inaccurate performance evaluation.

By examining the implications of multiperiod incentive contracts, Murphy sheds some light on the pay-for-performance controversy. His results suggest that the relation between pay and performance is significantly stronger during an executive's initial years with the firm as CEO than in later years.[117] This implies that there is a need to examine this relationship longitudinally in the future.

Along these same lines, Ungson and Steers cite contemporary examples in present-day corporations that suggest that compensation appears to be a function of size, inversely related to performance, or used as a protective cushion or reward paid in the event of failure, not success.[118] In order to reconcile these puzzling realities with theory they suggest that the role of motivation and politics in the determination of compensation be examined in future work. With regards to potential moderating variables to be examined, they cite the influence of owner control and corporate strategy as providing a potential link between compensation and rewards. Furthermore, by adopting a political perspective as opposed to the functional-rational approach utilized in the past, greater insights into why there exists such disparity between compensation and performance may be gained. Such a political perspective of executive compensation would be based on the following propositions: (1) CEO rewards may be more a function of political rather than economic factors; (2) the time-frame of rewards is in fact more ambiguous than the typically employed one- to three-year span; (3) a more comprehensive typology of rewards is needed to include intangible features of the job; and (4) the relationship between the CEO and the CEO's evaluators (the board of directors) is an important context along with firm- and industry-specific variables in analyzing executive compensation.

In summary and looking to the future, Finkelstein and Hambrick suggest an agenda for future research in the area of executive compensation.[119] Comprehending executive compensation will necessitate the use of multiple perspectives—economic, political, social, and individual—and concentration on both determinants and consequences of executive compensation contracts. In particular, there is a need to differentiate between the mix and type of pay. Do tax implications and fashion play a role in determining compensation schemes, and if so, what are the implications in terms of firm performance? In the area of determinants, discretion, industry factors, CEO tenure/age, and diversification should be explored. The possible link between compensation and diversification activity is based on findings indicating that bigger firms pay more, and therefore provide an incentive for CEOs to diversify. Compensation policies may drive diversification activities and is certainly an important question to consider.

NOTES

1. George P. Baker, Michael C. Jensen, and Kevin J. Murphy, "Compensation and Incentives: Practice vs. Theory," *Journal of Finance* 42/3 (1988): 593–94.

2. S. Finkelstein and D. C. Hambrick, "Chief Executive Compensation: A Synthesis and Reconciliation," *Strategic Management Journal* 9 (1988): 544.

3. Baker, Jensen, and Murphy, "Compensation and Incentives," p. 612.

4. Ibid.

5. Ibid.

6. Ibid.

7. See William J. Baumol, *Business Behavior, Value and Growth* (New York: Harcourt, Brace and World, 1967); R. Marris, *The Economic Theory of Managerial Capitalism* (London: Macmillan, 1964); and G. Yarrow, "Executive Compensation and the Objectives of the Firm," in *Market Structure and Corporate Behavior*, ed. K. Cowling (London: Gray-Mills, 1972).

8. See K. Arrow, "Higher Education as a Filter," *Journal of Public Economics* (July 1973): 193–216; J. E. Stiglitz, "The Theory of 'Screening,' Education, and the Distribution of Income," *American Economic Review* (June 1975): 283–305; P. J. Taubman and T. Wales, "Higher Education, Mental Ability, and Screening," *Journal of Political Economy* (Jan./Feb. 1973): 28–55; and K. Wolpin, "Education and Screening," *American Economic Review* (Dec. 1977): 949–58.

9. See L. C. Thurow, *Generalizing Inequality* (New York: Basic Books, 1975).

10. See G. Becker, *Human Capital* (New York: National Bureau of Economic Research, 1964).

11. The dual theory and the radical theory of segmented labor markets have more relevance to labor in general than to executive compensation. See Glen C. Cain, "The Challenge of Segmented Labor Market Theories to Orthodox Theory: A Survey," *Journal of Economic Literature* 14/4 (Dec. 1976): 1215–57, for a review.

12. Timothy D. Hogan and Lee R. McPheters, "Executive Compensation: Performance versus Personal Characteristics," *Southern Economic Journal* 46 (1980): 1067.

13. Naresh C. Agarwal, "Determinants of Executive Compensation," *Industrial Relations* 20/1 (1981): 36–46.

14. Ibid., p. 38.

15. Ibid., p. 39.

16. Becker, *Human Capital*.

17. Agarwal, "Determinants of Executive Compensation," p. 39.

18. See M. Jensen and W. H. Meckling, "Theory of the Firm and Managerial Behavior, Agency Costs, and Ownership Structure," *Journal of Financial Economics* 3 (1976): 305–60; Richard A. Lambert and David F. Larker, "Executive Compensation, Corporate Decision-Making and Shareholder Wealth: A Review of the Evidence," *Midland Corporate Finance Journal* (Winter 1985): 6–22; and C. Smith and R. Watts, "Incentive and Tax Effects of Executive Compensation Plans," *Australian Journal of Management* 7 (1982): 139–57.

19. B. Holmstrom, "Moral Hazard and Observability," *Bell Journal of Economics* 10 (1979): 74–91.

20. S. Butler and M. Maher, *Management Incentive Compensation Plans* (Montvale, N.J.: NAA, 1986).

21. Smith and Watts, "Incentive and Tax Effects of Executive Compensation Plans," p. 156.

22. See Ross L. Watts and Jerold L. Zimmerman, *Positive Accounting Theory* (Englewood Cliffs, N.J.: Prentice-Hall, 1986).

23. Smith and Watts, "Incentive and Tax Effects of Executive Compensation Plans," p. 146.

24. M. P. Narayanan, "Managerial Incentives for Short-term Results," *Journal of Finance* 40/5 (1985): 1469–84.

25. Ibid., p. 1469.

26. Mary W. O'Keefe, Kip Viscusi, and Richard J. Zeckhauser, "Economic Contests: Comparative Reward Schemes," *Journal of Labor Economics* 2/1 (1984): 28.

27. Charles A. O'Reilly, III, Brian G. Main, and Graef S. Crystal, "CEO Compensation as Tournament and Social Comparison: A Tale of Two Theories," *Administrative Science Quarterly* 33 (1988): 260.

28. Edward P. Lazear and Sherwin Rosen, "Rank-order Tournaments as Optimum Labor Contracts," *Journal of Political Economy* 89/51 (1981): 841–64.

29. Ibid., p. 847.

30. O'Reilly, Main, and Crystal, "CEO Compensation as Tournament and Social Comparison," p. 262.

31. See Holmstrom, "Moral Hazard and Observability"; and Richard A. Lambert and David F. Larker, "An Analysis of the Use of Accounting and Market Measures of Performance in Executive Compensation Contracts," *Journal of Accounting Research* 25 (Supplement 1987): 85–129.

32. R. Antle and A. Smith, "An Empirical Investigation of the Relative Performance Evaluation of Corporate Executives," *Journal of Accounting Research* 24/1 (1986): 7.

33. Ibid.

34. Ibid.

35. See Baumol, *Business Behavior, Value and Growth,* for a discussion.

36. W. G. Lewellen and B. Huntsman, "Managerial Pay and Corporate Performance," *American Economic Review* (Sept. 1970): 710.

37. See Antle and Smith, "Empirical Investigation of the Relative Performance Evaluation of Corporate Executives"; or Lambert and Larker, "Analysis of the Use of Accounting and Market Measures of Performance in Executive Compensation Contracts."

38. See G. Benston, "The Self-Serving Management Hypothesis: Some Evidence," *Journal of Accounting and Economics* (Apr. 1985): 67–84; Allen and Hamilton Booz, *Executive Pay in the Eighties: Major Exposures Ahead* (New York: Booz, Allen and Hamilton, 1983); and Hay Associates, "Fifth Annual Hay Report on Executive Compensation," *Wharton Magazine* (Apr. 1985): 85–107.

39. M. Jensen and K. Murphy, "Are Executive Compensation Contracts Structured Properly?" (working paper, University of Rochester, 1987).

40. Joseph W. McGuire, John S. Chiu, and Alvar O. Elbing, "Executive Incomes, Sales and Profits," *American Economic Review* (Sept. 1962): 760.

41. Lewellen and Huntsman, "Managerial Pay and Corporate Performance."

42. Ibid., p. 13.

43. R. T. Masson, "Executive Motivations, Earnings and Consequent Equity Performance," *Journal of Political Economy* (Dec. 1971): 1281.

44. A. Cosh, "The Remuneration of Chief Executives in the United Kingdom," *Economics Journal* 85 (Mar. 1975): 75–94.

45. Ibid., p. 90.

46. D. Ciscel and T. Carroll, "The Determinants of Executive Salaries: An Econometric Survey," *Review of Economics and Statistics* (Feb. 1980): 7–13.

47. Ibid., p. 13.

48. Hogan and McPheters, "Executive Compensation."

49. Agarwal, "Determinants of Executive Compensation."

50. Mark Hirschey and J. L. Pappas, "Regulatory and Life Cycle Influences on Managerial Incentives," *Southern Economic Journal* 48 (1981): 327–34.

51. Ibid., p. 334.

52. Kevin Murphy, "Corporate Performance and Managerial Remuneration: An Empirical Analysis," *Journal of Accounting and Economics* (Apr. 1985): 11–42.

53. Ibid., p. 40.

54. Lambert and Larker, "Analysis of the Use of Accounting and Market Measures of Performance in Executive Compensation Contracts," p. 96.

55. Antle and Smith, "Empirical Investigation of the Relative Performance Evaluation of Corporate Executives."

56. Ibid., p. 32.

57. L. Gomez-Mejia, H. Tosi, and T. Hinkin, "Managerial Control, Performance and Executive Compensation," *Academy of Management Journal* 30 (1987): 51–70.

58. Ibid., p. 51.

59. W. G. Lewellen, C. Loderer, and K. Martin, "Executive Compensation and Executive Incentive Problems: An Empirical Analysis," *Journal of Accounting and Economics* 9 (1987): 287–310.

60. Ibid., p. 287.

61. John R. Deckop, "Determinants of Chief Executive Officer Compensation," *Industrial and Labor Relations Review* 41/2 (1988): 215–26.

62. Ibid., p. 225.

63. K. Ely, "Cross-sectional Variations in the Relationship Between Accounting Variables and the Chief Executive's Compensation," (working paper, University of Chicago, 1988), p. 43.

64. Robert Gibbons and Kevin Murphy, "Relative Performance Evaluation for Chief Executive Officers," in *Do Compensation Policies Matter?* ed. Ronald G. Ehrenberg (Ithaca, N.Y.: ILR, 1990), pp. 30–51.

65. Ibid., p. 48.

66. Jonathan S. Leonard, "Executive Pay and Firm Performance," in *Do Compensation Policies Matter?*, ed. Ronald G. Ehrenberg (Ithaca, N.Y.: ILR, 1990), p. 18.

67. John M. Abowd, "Does Performance-Based Managerial Compensation Affect Corporate Performance?" in *Do Compensation Policies Matter?*, ed. Ronald G. Ehrenberg (Ithaca, N.Y.: ILR, 1990), pp. 52–73.

68. Ahmed Belkaoui, "Executive Compensation, Organizational Effectiveness, Social Performance and Firm Performance: An Empirical Investigation," *Journal of Business Finance and Accounting* (forthcoming).

69. Finkelstein and Hambrick, "Chief Executive Compensation," p. 549.

70. Masson, "Executive Motivations, Earnings and Consequent Equity Performance."

71. Ibid., pp. 1286–87.

72. D. Larker, "The Association Between Performance Plan Adoption and Corporate Capital Investment," *Journal of Accounting and Economics* (Apr. 1983): 27.

73. J. A. Brickley, S. Bhagat, and R. C. Lease, "The Impact of Long-Range Managerial Compensation Plans on Shareholder Wealth," *Journal of Accounting and Economics* 7 (1985): 115–29.

74. Michael S. Long, "The Incentives behind the Adoption of Executive Stock Option Plans in U.S. Corporations," (working paper, University of Illinois at Chicago 1988), p. 1.

75. Hassan Tehranian and J. F. Waegelein, "Market Reaction to Short-term Executive Compensation Plan Adoption," *Journal of Accounting and Economics* 7 (1985): 131–44.

76. James F. Waegelein, "The Association Between the Adoption of Short-Term Bonus Plans and Corporate Expenditures," *Journal of Accounting and Public Policy* 7 (1988): 43–63.

77. Ibid., p. 61.

78. Richard A. Lambert and David F. Larker, "Golden Parachutes, Executive Decision-Making, and Shareholder Wealth," *Journal of Accounting and Economics* 7 (1985): 201.

79. Lawrence W. Kahn and Peter D. Sherer, "Contingent Pay and Managerial Performance," in *Do Compensation Policies Matter?*, ed. Ronald G. Ehrenberg (Ithaca, N.Y.: ILR, 1990), pp. 107–20.

80. Ibid., pp. 109–10.

81. Watts and Zimmerman, *Positive Accounting Theory*, p. 208.

82. R. M. Bowen, E. W. Noreen, and J. M. Lacey, "Determinants of the Corporate Decision to Capitalize Interest," *Journal of Accounting and Economics* 3/2 (1981): 153.

83. Paul M. Healy, "The Effect of Bonus Schemes on Accounting Decisions," *Journal of Accounting and Economics* 7 (1985): 85–107.

84. Ibid., p. 106.

85. Maureen McNichols and G. Peter Wilson, "Evidence of Earnings Management from the Provision for Bad Debts," (working paper, Stanford University, 1988).

86. Ibid., p. 28.

87. Paul M. Healy, S. Kang, and K. Palepu, "The Effect of Accounting Procedure Changes on CEOs Cash Salary and Bonus Compensation," *Journal of Accounting and Economics* 9 (1987): 7–34.

88. A. R. Abdel-Khalik, Charles Chiu, and Dimitrios Ghicas, "Rationality of Executive Compensation Schemes and Real Accounting Changes," *Contemporary Accounting Research* 4/1 (1987): 32–60.

89. Healy, Kang, and Palepu, "Effect of Accounting Procedure Changes," p. 7.

90. Abdel-Khalik, Chiu, and Ghicas, "Rationality of Executive Compensation Schemes and Real Accounting Changes," p. 58.

91. W. G. Lewellen, C. Loderer, and A. Rosenfeld, "Merger Decisions and Executive Stock Ownership in Acquiring Firms," *Journal of Accounting and Economics* 7 (1985): 209–31.

92. Ibid., p. 230.

93. Richard A. Lambert and David J. Larker, "Executive Compensation Effects of Large Corporate Acquisitions," *Journal of Accounting and Public Policy* 6 (1987): 231–43.

94. H. Tehranian, N. Travlos, and J. F. Waegelein, "Management Compensation

Contracts and Merger-induced Abnormal Returns,'' *Journal of Accounting Research* 25 (Supplement 1987): 51–76.

95. Ibid., p. 74.

96. See Lambert and Larker, ''Executive Compensation, Corporate Decision-Making and Shareholder Wealth,'' pp. 15–17, for a discussion of the labor market for executives.

97. Finkelstein and Hambrick, ''Chief Executive Compensation,'' p. 546.

98. Ibid., p. 547.

99. Benston, ''Self-Serving Management Hypothesis,'' p. 67.

100. A. Coughlin and R. Schmidt, ''Executive Compensation, Management Turnover, and Firm Performance: An Empirical Investigation,'' *Journal of Accounting and Economics* (Apr. 1985): 43–66.

101. Jeffrey Kerr and Richard A. Bettis, ''Boards of Directors, Top Management Compensation, and Shareholder Returns,'' *Academy of Management Journal* 30/4 (1987): 645–64.

102. Ibid., p. 658.

103. W. Bruce Johnson et al., ''An Analysis of the Stock Price Reaction to Sudden Executive Deaths: Implications for the Managerial Labor Market,'' *Journal of Accounting and Economics* 7 (1985): 151–74.

104. Ibid., p. 155.

105. Lambert and Larker, ''Executive Compensation Effects of Large Corporate Acquisitions.''

106. G. R. Salancik and J. Pfeffer, ''The Effects of Ownership and Performance on Executive Tenure in U.S. Corporations,'' *Academy of Management Journal* 23 (1980): 653–64.

107. O'Reilly, Main, and Crystal, ''CEO Compensation as Tournament and Social Comparison.''

108. Ronald G. Ehrenberg and Michael L. Bognanno, ''The Incentive Effects of Tournaments Revisited: Evidence from the European PGA Tour,'' in *Do Compensation Policies Matter?,* ed. Ronald G. Ehrenberg (Ithaca, N.Y.: ILR, 1990), pp. 74–88.

109. Ibid., p. 87.

110. Hogan and McPheters, ''Executive Compensation,'' p. 1067.

111. Gomez-Mejia, Tosi, and Hinkin, ''Managerial Control, Performance, and Executive Compensation,'' p. 65.

112. Salancik and Pfeffer, ''Effects of Ownership and Performance on Executive Tenure in U.S. Corporations.''

113. See Finkelstein and Hambrick, ''Chief Executive Compensation,'' for a discussion.

114. Coughlin and Schmidt, ''Executive Compensation, Management Turnover, and Firm Performance.''

115. Henry L. Tosi and Luis R. Gomez-Mejia, ''The Decoupling of CEO Pay and Performance: An Agency Theory Perspective,'' *Administrative Science Quarterly* 34 (1989): 169–89.

116. See Baker, Jensen, and Murphy, ''Compensation and Incentives'' for a discussion.

117. K. Murphy, ''Incentives, Learning, and Compensation: A Theoretical and Empirical Investigation of Managerial Labor Contracts,'' *Rand Journal of Economics* 17 (Spring 1986): 59–76.

118. Gerardo Ungson and Richard Steers, "Motivation and Politics in Executive Compensation," *Academy of Management Review* 9/2 (1984): 313–23.
119. Finkelstein and Hambrick, "Chief Executive Compensation."

REFERENCES

Abdel-Khalik, A. R., Charles Chiu, and Dimitrios Ghicas. 1987. Rationality of executive compensation schemes and real accounting changes. *Contemporary Accounting Research* 4 (1): 32–60.

Abowd, John M. 1990. Does performance-based managerial compensation affect subsequent corporate performance? In *Do Compensation Policies Matter?* ed. Ronald G. Ehrenberg. pp. 52–73. Ithaca, N.Y.: ILR Press.

Agarwal, Naresh C. 1981. Determinants of executive compensation. *Industrial Relations* 20 (1): 36–46.

Antle, R. and Smith, A. 1986. An empirical investigation of the relative performance evaluation of corporate executives. *Journal of Accounting Research* 24 (1): 1–39.

Belkaoui, A. 1990. Executive compensation, organizational effectiveness, social performance and firm performance: An empirical investigation. *Journal of Business Finance and Accounting* (forthcoming).

Benston, G. 1985. The self-serving hypothesis: Some evidence. *Journal of Accounting and Economics* (April): 67–84.

Bowen, R. M., Noreen, E. W. and Lacey, J. M. 1981. Determinants of the corporate decision to capitalize interest. *Journal of Accounting and Economics* 3 (2): 151–179.

Brickley, J. A., S. Bhagat and R. C. Lease. 1985. The impact of long-range managerial compensation plans on shareholder wealth. *Journal of Accounting and Economics* 7: 115–129.

Ciscel, D. and Carroll T. 1980. The determinants of executive salaries: An econometric survey. *Review of Economics and Statistics* (February): 7–13.

Cosh, A. 1975. The remuneration of chief executives in the United Kingdom. *Economics Journal* 85 (March): 75–94.

Coughlin, A. and Schmidt, R. 1985. Executive compensation, management turnover, and firm performance: An empirical investigation. *Journal of Accounting and Economics* (April): 43–66.

Deckop, John R. 1988. Determinants of chief executive officer compensation. *Industrial and Labor Relations Review* 41 (2): 215–226.

Ehrenberg, Ronald G. and Borgnanno. 1990. The incentive effects of tournaments revisited: Evidence from the European PGA tour. In *Do Compensation Policies Matter?* ed. Ronald G. Ehrenberg. pp. 74–88. Ithaca, NY: ILR Press.

Ely, K. 1988. Cross-sectional variations in the relationship between accounting variables and the chief executive's compensation. Working Paper. University of Chicago.

Gibbons, Robert and Murphy, Kevin. 1990. Relative performance evaluation for chief executive officers. In *Do Compensation Policies Matter?*, ed. Ronald G. Ehrenberg. pp. 30–51. Ithaca, NY: ILR Press.

Gomez-Mejia, L., Tosi, H. and Hinkin, T. 1987. Managerial control, performance and executive compensation. *Academy of Management Journal* 30: 51–70.

Healy, Paul M. 1985. The effect of bonus schemes on accounting decisions. *Journal of Accounting and Economics* 7: 85–107.

Healy, Paul M., S. Kang and K. Palepu. 1987. The effect of accounting procedure changes on CEOs' cash salary and bonus compensation. *Journal of Accounting and Economics* 9: 7–34.

Hirschey, Mark and J. L. Pappas. 1981. Regulatory and life cycle influences on managerial incentives. *Southern Economic Journal* 48: 327–332.

Hogan, T. and L. McPheters. 1980. Executive compensation: Performance versus personal characteristics. *Southern Economic Journal* 46: 1060–1068.

Johnson, W. Bruce, Robert P. Magee, N. Nagarajan and Harry A. Newman. 1985. An analysis of the stock price reaction to sudden executive deaths: Implications for the managerial labor market. *Journal of Accounting and Economics* 7: 151–174.

Kahn, Lawrence W. and Sherer, Peter D. 1990. Contingent pay and managerial performance. In *Do Compensation Policies Matter?* ed. Ronald G. Ehrenberg. pp. 107–120. Ithaca, NY: ILR Press.

Kerr, Jeffrey and Richard A. Bettis. 1987. Boards of directors, top management compensation, and shareholder returns. *Academy of Management Journal* 30 (4): 645–664.

Lambert, Richard A. and David F. Larker. 1985. Golden parachutes, executive decision-making, and shareholder wealth. *Journal of Accounting and Economics* 7: 179–203.

———. 1985. Executive compensation, corporate decision-making and shareholder wealth: A review of the evidence. *Midland Corporate Finance Journal* (Winter): 6–22.

———. 1987. Executive compensation effects of large corporate acquisitions. *Journal of Accounting and Public Policy* 6: 231–243.

———. 1987. An analysis of the use of accounting and market measures of performance in executive compensation contracts. *Studies in Stewardship Uses of Accounting Information, Supplement to the Journal of Accounting Research* 25: 85–129.

Larker, D. 1983. The association between performance plan adoption and corporate capital investment. *Journal of Accounting and Economics* (April): 3–30.

Leonard, Jonathan S. 1990. Executive pay and firm performance. In *Do Compensation Policies Matter,* ed. Ronald G. Ehrenberg. pp. 13–29. Ithaca, NY: ILR Press.

Lewellen, W. G. and Huntsman, B. 1970. Managerial pay and corporate performance. *American Economic Review* (September): 710–720.

Lewellen, W. G., C. Loderer and K. Martin. 1987. Executive compensation and executive incentive problems An empirical analysis. *Journal of Accounting and Economics* 9: 287–310.

Lewellen, W. G., C. Loderer and A. Rosenfeld. 1985. Merger decisions and executive stock ownership in acquiring firms. *Journal of Accounting and Economics* 7: 209–231.

Long, Michael S. 1988. The incentives behind the adoption of executive stock option plans in U.S. corporations. Working Paper. University of Illinois at Chicago.

Masson, R. T. 1971. Executive motivations, earnings and consequent equity performance. *Journal of Political Economy* (December): 1278–1292.

McGuire, J., J. Chiu and A. Elbing. 1962. Executive incomes, sales and profits. *American Economic Review* (September): 753–761.

McNichols, Maureen and G. Peter Wilson. 1988. Evidence of earnings management from the provision for bad debts. Working Paper. Stanford University, Stanford, California.

Murphy, Kevin. 1985. Corporate performance and managerial remuneration: An empirical analysis. *Journal of Accounting and Economics* (April): 11–42.

O'Reilly, Charles A., III, Brian G. Main and Graef S. Crystal. 1988. CEO compensation as tournament and social comparison: A tale of two theories. *Administrative Science Quarterly* 33: 257–274.

Salancik, G. R. and J. Pfeffer. 1980 The effects of ownership and performance on executive tenure in U.S. corporations. *Academy of Management Journal* 23: 653–664.

Tehranian, Hassan, and J. F. Waegelein. 1985. Market reaction to short-term executive compensation plan adoption. *Journal of Accounting and Economics* 7: 131–144.

Waegelein, James F. 1988. The association between the adoption of short-term bonus plans and corporate expenditures. *Journal of Accounting and Public Policy* 7: 43–63.

2

THE MULTIDIVISIONAL HYPOTHESIS

The multidivisional form of organization (m-form) has been favored among large firms in the U.S. economy. This significant organizational innovation, developed in the 1920s, "was little noted and not widely appreciated . . . as late as 1960. Leading management texts extolled the virtues of 'basic departmentation' and 'line and staff authority relationships' but the special importance of multidivisionalization went unremarked."[1] By definition, the m-form has as one of its key elements a separation of strategic decision making from operating decision making. Historically, "the M-form structure fashioned by du Pont and Sloan involved the creation of semiautonomous operating divisions (mainly profit centers) organized along product, brand, or geographic lines. The operating affairs of each were managed separately."[2]

Why do so many firms adopt this particular form of organization? What are the ramifications of the m-form structure in terms of firm performance, policies, and decision making? The literature suggests adoption of the m-form may be viewed as an adaptive organizational response. It is the purpose of this chapter to examine more thoroughly these questions.

THEORETICAL EXPLANATIONS

The multidivisional form has been explained by five theories in the literature: (1) strategy-structure; (2) transaction cost analysis; (3) population-ecology theory; (4) control theory based on power; and (5) organizational homogeneity theory. As Fligstein comments,

If the theories . . . are to prove useful, then they should allow us to explain the dissemination of this important organizational innovation. This is not to say that the differences between these theories are small. In fact the theories are based on quite different assumptions about the power, constraints, and rationality of key actors in large organizations.[3]

Strategy and Structure

Alfred Chandler was responsible for the initial insights of strategy-structure theory.[4] According to Chandler, "corporate structure refers to the design of the organization and it includes the lines of communication and authority between administrative offices as well as the information that flows between them."[5] The functional aspect of organizational structure involves major subunits of a business that deal with business functions such as sales, engineering, and production, while the multidivisional aspect involves the splitting of the organization into semiautonomous operating units by product or geographic region.

There are obviously many other ways to classify or categorize organizational structures that in turn describe the relationship between a central office and its various subunits.[6] Chandler theorizes that a firm's structure is a response to its pursuit of a particular strategy that is defined as "the determination of the long-term goals and objectives of an enterprise, and the adoption of courses of action and the allocation of resources necessary for carrying out those goals."[7] In other words, strategy determines structure. Chandler delineates three basic strategies: (1) horizontal (implying expansion in geographic markets); (2) vertical (backwards or forwards); and (3) diversification into related or unrelated product groups. Chandler asserts that a horizontal strategy will result in a unitary structure (the organization will be divided functionally into manufacturing, sales, and finance); a vertical strategy will result in a functional structure wherein tasks are the basis for departmentalization; and a diversification strategy will lead to a multidivisional structure characterized by decentralized management and product divisions organized in a unitary fashion.

Chandler's theory of why firms adopt a diversification strategy in the first place keys in on the concept of a firm's response to a changing environment and its desire to exploit that new environment by utilizing already existing technology. In other words, certain firms with certain technologies that are congruent with related or unrelated product production are more likely to adopt a diversification strategy in response to environmental change.

For example, firms with knowledge in electrical science first concentrated on creating capital goods for the generation of power. Widespread electrification led to consumer and industrial products that utilized electrical motors as power sources. Firms possessing skill in electrical knowledge were able to diversify into a number of related businesses, including radios, television, transistors, and computers. Likewise firms possessing expertise in chemical science have been able to apply their technology in such diverse businesses as textiles and antibiotics. Once the decision to diversify has been made, the m-form structure becomes an efficient choice in the management of different product lines. According to Chandler, "the basic reason for its success was simply that it clearly removed the executives responsible for the destiny of the entire enterprise from the more routine operational activities, and so gave them the time, information, and even psychological commitment for long-term planning and appraisal."[8]

Transaction Cost Analysis

Williamson, building on the work of Chandler, also acknowledges the difficulties encountered by a unitary-form (u-form) enterprise faced with expansion.[9] The u-form of organization, a prevalent organizational structure prior to the 1920s, is one in which the firm is divided into manufacturing, sales and marketing, and finance departments. Williamson theorizes that in u-form firms adopting diversification strategies

the ability of the management to handle the volume and complexity of the demands placed upon it became strained and even collapsed. Unable meaningfully to identify with or contribute to the realization of global goals, managers in each of the functional parts attended to what they perceived to be operational subgoals instead.[10]

In other words, these difficulties centering around "control loss" effects are consequences of bounded rationality and opportunism, two of the basic tenets of transaction cost economics.

According to Williamson, the rationale behind the multifunction firm rests on incomplete information, transaction costs, and uncertainty. Transaction costs are defined as the costs of performing an exchange transaction. Transaction cost economics views human nature as subject to bounded rationality and opportunistic behavior. Bounded rationality and opportunistic behavior relate to assumptions regarding individual agents. Bounded rationality implies that there are "bounds on the rate at which information can be absorbed per unit of time, limits to the information storage capacity (in an effective retrieval sense), and bounds on the processing ability of the decision-maker."[11] Opportunistic behavior is expressed when individuals act in their own self-interest even when their actions are contrary to the interests of the firm. Opportunistic behavior is "a condition of self-interest seeking with guile."[12]

In the case of an expanding firm, Williamson argues that a functionally organized firm will experience "cumulative control losses" resulting in inefficiency. At the same time, individual actors will reach their limit with respect to control, due to bounded rationality, and opportunistic behavior will be observed. "In the language of transaction cost economics, bounds of rationality were reached as the U-form structure labored under a communication overload while the pursuit of subgoals by the functional parts (sales, engineering, production) was partly a manifestation of opportunism."[13]

In short, profitability and continued growth of the firm will be threatened. If costs of transacting with the outside market are high, continued growth of the firm and a resolution of the control and efficiency problems may be accomplished by adoption of the m-form structure. To be efficient, an organization must "economize" on bounded rationality, which is accomplished with the m-form structure by assigning transactions to governing structures (i.e., hierarchies) in a discriminating way. To summarize, firms choose to participate in outside markets or establish hierarchies internally in dealing with tasks on the basis of transaction costs and opportunistic behavior. When a company diverts from the u-form of structure, control loss problems occur due to bounded rationality. If opportunistic behavior is assumed and transaction costs are high, the organization establishes hierarchies (to govern) as a means of resolving control problems and promoting both efficiency and profitability. The m-form structure is a manifestation of this process. Williamson's work in this area resulted in his formulation of what is known as the m-form hypothesis:

The organization and operation of the large enterprise along the lines of the M-Form (Multidivisional form) favors goal-pursuit and least-cost behavior more nearly associated with the neoclassical profit-maximization hypothesis than does the U-Form (functional form) organization structure.[14]

Population-Ecology Theory

Sociologists are also concerned with the question of organizational structure. Although the m-form is not dealt with directly, one sociological school of thought, population-ecology theory, provides some insights into why organizations adopt and cling to a particular structure. At an industry level it is theorized that organizations choose and continue with structures that may have been appropriate for social conditions existing when the industry was founded, even though these conditions no longer exist. These structures "tend to become institutionalized over time, because the efficiency characteristics of alternative structures are often difficult and sometimes impossible to assess. Firms cope with this uncertainty, and in the process obtain legitimacy, by simply adopting the structure that is most popular and normatively prescribed at the moment."[15]

Hannan and Freeman, in an organizational-level view of population-ecology theory, assert that there exists a relationship among organizational niche, age, inertia, and the possibility of organizational change.[16] Their theory further asserts that as organizations age, they tend to stay the same structurally—a concept aptly called structural inertia. It is thought that it is the environment surrounding organizations that provides a selection device. That is, the environment determines which firms will continue and which will fall to the wayside. As corporations grow, age, and survive the selection process, the risks and costs involved in attempting organizational change become greater. The implication for adoption of the m-form structure derived from this theory is that "younger and smaller firms would be more likely to adopt the M-Form than older and larger ones."[17]

Control Theory

Control theory focuses on the individual participants (actors) who possess economic power in an organization. Economic power in an organization lies in the ability to influence decisions concerning allocation of scarce resources. Hence, organizational decisions, for example, the choice of strategy or structure, may be influenced by those individuals in control of scarce resources. But which personnel group is dominant or has the power in an organization? If the dominant actors are from sales and marketing, this theory would argue that a product-related strategy would be adopted that would result in a consistent organizational structure, namely, the m-form.

From the power perspective, the multidivisional form would result from the acts of certain key actors whose strategic bases of power are consistent with the multidivisional form. Since the multidivisional form could be viewed as a mechanism which allows for growth through product-related and unrelated strategies, its implementation would be favored by . . . sales personnel.[18]

The adoption of the m-form structure in turn leads to a further entrenchment of the power of these particular actors.

Power or control in a corporation has also been hypothesized to be influenced by the ownership structure of the corporation. Palmer et al. argue that "the more a firm's stock is dispersed among many unrelated individuals or corporations that do not have representatives in top management or on the board, the more control is separated from ownership and placed in the hands of management."[19] Furthermore, "ownership represents a source of power that can be used either to support or oppose management depending on how it is concentrated and used."[20] Palmer et al. suggest that the higher the concentration of stock in the hands of a few individuals, the less likelihood of adoption of the multidivisional form. In fact, "family-dominated firms will resist adopting the multidivisional form, because family coalitions prefer centralized organizational structures that allow them to control the day-to-day affairs of the firms in which they have an interest."[21]

Organizational Homogeneity Theory

A final theoretical argument for the genesis of the m-form of organization is espoused by what is known as the organization homogeneity perspective. It is based on the notion that organizations tend to mimic or resemble other organizations. The process that leads to this homogeneity may be viewed as follows. First, an organization may use a particular structure initially as an appropriate response to social conditions existing when the industry is founded. This structure may tend to become "institutionalized" over time. The "worldview" of managers in a particular industry may promote this homogeneity. In summary, this theory asserts that a "bandwagon effect" may result when other organizations flock to adopt a particular structural form (i.e., m-form) due to other companies' prior success. Historically, "the MDF spreads to various organizations as a response to other firms' behavior. The examples of successful firms such as DuPont or General Motors provided the role models for other firms."[22] It has even been suggested that business school education may be a causal factor in the proliferation of diversification strategies and the multidivisional form of organization.

Summary of Multiproduct Firm Theories

Fligstein tested the assumptions of the previously noted theories in an attempt to model the adoption of the m-form and organizational change in general. The evidence suggests three things:

1. Actors in the organization interpret the environment, and in doing so are not necessarily rational, in that "actors cannot be assumed to understand what is occurring in the internal and external environments."[23]
2. Actors' interpretations reflect their own positions in the organization, and thus "the interpretations of key organizational problems may themselves be constructions."[24]
3. In order to enforce their solutions to organizational problems, actors must have some resource base either within the organization or the environment.[25]

On a final note, "organizational change may or may not aid the organization in surviving. In the case of firms, actors must be oriented toward profit-making, but there are many strategies that could aid or hinder that goal. In the end, the actions of key actors may or may not work to preserve the organization."[26] It is these strategies and their effect on the performance of the firm that will be examined in the next section.

Additional contributions to multiproduct firm theory have been made by Teece, who argues that the transaction cost literature has "made it possible to outline a theory of the multiproduct firm. Important building blocks include excess capacity and its creation, market imperfections, and the peculiarities of organizational knowledge, particularly its fungibility and tacit character."[27] With regard to excess capacity, a firm can be envisioned to have the following choices: sell unused resources to other firms, diversify, or reinvest in their traditional business. According to Teece, a theory of diversification emerges when the second option maximizes profit. "The first option involves the use of markets for capturing the employment value of the unused assets. Multiproduct diversification (option 2) will be selected by profit seeking firms over the market alternative (option 1) when transactions cost problems are likely to confound efficient transfer."[28]

Palmer et al. found support for the Chandler and Williamson theories, which are often referred to as economic explanations, but concluded that they were insufficient. The basic thrust of the economic explanations of multiproduct firms is that firms choose organizational structures that maximize efficiency and in turn profitability. Accordingly, "if firms pursuing complex strategies retain the U-form or firms pursuing simple strategies adopt the M-form, their profitability will decline and they will die or be acquired (and presumably reorganized.)"[29]

Ecological and political theories were found to provide additional explanatory power. According to these theories individual actors that engage in transactions are also linked by social structures. "These social structures are important. . . . They may cause actors to pursue interests other than those related to the efficiency of the transactions in which they are involved when choosing between alternative transaction modes, even at the expense of those transactions' efficiency." [30]

To summarize, any future comprehensive theory of the multidivisional firm must include consideration of economic, political, ecological, geographical, and behavioral factors. Further research in each of these areas is needed to provide us with a more complete knowledge of the incentives for diversification and the adoption of the multidivisional form of organization.

FIRM STRUCTURE, DIVERSIFICATION STRATEGIES, PERFORMANCE, AND MEASUREMENT

Structure, Diversification, and Performance: A Categorical Approach

In order to study the m-form of organization, strategy, and performance, various measures of diversification have been proposed. Rumelt finds

that firms varied not only in terms of absolute product diversity but in the patterns of relationships that they established among different lines of business. Interestingly, it was also found that corporate profitability differed significantly across groups of firms following different "strategies" of diversification. [31]

Rumelt seeks to explore the idea that "organizational structure is intimately related to a firm's strategy of expansion." [32] Therefore, he utilizes a subjective categorization of firms that includes both structural and strategic characteristics.

To gauge diversification strategy Rumelt utilizes the following ratios along with qualitative information about the firms in his study:

1. Specialization Ratio (SR): Proportion of a firm's revenue that is attributable to its largest discrete product-market activity. This ratio reflects a useful general measure of diversity.
2. Related Ratio (RR): Proportion of a firm's revenues that are attributable to its largest group of businesses related in some way to one another. This ratio distinguishes between firms employing related and unrelated diversification strategies.

To gauge structure Rumelt utilizes the following:

Vertical Ratio (VR): Proportion of a firm's revenues attributable to all of the by-products, intermediate products, and final products of a vertically integrated sequence of manufacturing operations.

Based upon the above ratios, firms are classified into one of the following diversification strategy categories (which also contain historical information based on Rumelt's[33] findings on organizational structure):

1. Single Business: $SR > .95$ (If nonvertical, $VR < .7$ and if vertically integrated, $VR > .7$)

Single businesses are viewed strategically as being devoted to one product and usually exhibit a u-form structure.

2. Dominant Business: $.7 < SR < .95$ (If nonvertical, $VR < .7$ and if vertically integrated, $VR > .7$)
   2A. Dominant Vertical: $VR > .7$
   2B. Dominant Constrained: Nonvertical built on a particular strength.
   2C. Dominant Linked: Nonvertical built on several strengths.
   2D. Dominant Unrelated: Nonvertical in which diversified activities are not related to the dominant business.

Dominant businesses in general are viewed as exhibiting a small degree of diversification, while still deriving the majority of their revenue from a single business. Those firms classified as dominant vertical during the period 1949–1969 were more likely to exhibit a u-form structure than the dominant constrained. However, by 1959 a majority of firms classified as either dominant linked or dominant unrelated had adopted a multidivisional structure.

3. Related Business: Nonvertical, $SR < .7$, $RR > .7$
   3A. Related Constrained: Have diversified into new businesses that are related to an existing skill or resource.
   3B. Related Linked: Diversified into new businesses related to existing skill or resource, but not always the same skill or resource leading to a wide diversity of businesses.

In general related businesses are nonvertically diversified firms that seek to capitalize on existing skills and resources. By 1959 a majority of firms in this category exhibited a multidivisional organizational structure.

4. Unrelated Business: Nonvertical, $RR < .7$
   4A. Unrelated Passive: Do not qualify as acquisitive conglomerate (see below).
   4B. Acquisitive Conglomerate: Firms aggressively pursuing the acquisition of new unrelated businesses.

Unrelated businesses have adopted a diversification policy that is not influenced by current activities or strengths. For the period 1949–1969, almost all unrelated diversifiers studied by Rumelt had adopted a multidivisional structure.

Rumelt finds that significant performance differences exist among his diversification strategy categories. Specifically, the Dominant-Constrained and Related Constrained groups were unquestionably the best overall performers, and both strategies are based on the concept of controlled diversity. Neither totally dependent upon a single business nor true multi-industry firms, these companies have strategies of entering only those businesses that build on . . . some central strength or competence.[34]

With regard to organizational structure, "firms with product-division structures had rates of growth that, on the average, were significantly higher than those of firms with other types of organizational structures. Their rates of profit were at least as high as those of other firms."[35]

The Decision to Diversify

According to Michel and Shaked, "the decision whether to diversify into related or unrelated business is primarily based on two conflicting considerations."[36] On the one hand, related diversification offers a firm an opportunity to create a certain synergism based on shared resources that in turn should enhance efficiency and profitability. On the other hand, unrelated diversification, while not likely to produce such synergism, may result in a total risk reduction for the firm. "Thus, a priori, the direction of change in risk-adjusted performance associated with related and unrelated diversification is ambiguous."[37]

A great deal of both theoretical and empirical research has focused on the effects of strategy and structure in terms of firm performance. One school of thought assumes that all firms structured along the lines of the m-form are homogeneous in their control arrangements and therefore only differences in firm strategies matter in explaining differences in firm performance. Others argue that substantial differences exist in terms of control among m-form firms and that both variations within the m-form structure and differences in firm strategies matter in terms of firm performance. Since both schools of thought recognize a role for diversification strategy it is worthwhile to examine the economic argument behind the main strategies most commonly adopted by m-form firms: vertical integration, related diversification, and unrelated diversification.

Hill and Hoskisson attribute the economic benefit derived from vertical integration to a realization of increased value-added margins arising "from scale or integration economies as well as from [an] increase in control over sources of raw materials or over outlets.[38] Diversification into related businesses produces a synergistic effect resulting from shared inputs, known as economies of scope. Although a universally accepted theory of the economic benefits accruing to unrelated diversification has not been developed, it appears that these benefits are associated with what is known as exploiting financial economies as opposed to economies of scope or scale. It has been suggested that unrelated diversification can overcome external capital market failures. Often investors are at a disadvantage in their relationship with the firm due to their external position in circumstances where separation of ownership and control apply. As an internal investor, the head office of the firm that follows a strategy of unrelated diversification can overcome these.[39]

Alternative Measurements of Diversification

In order to assess the relationship among structure, strategy, and firm performance, other measurements of diversification strategy, besides the categorical one utilized by Rumelt, have been proposed. Even he admits that "there is no generally accepted definition or measure of diversification."[40] In essence there are two basic ways of conceptualizing and measuring diversification-business count measures and strategy-based measures. Business count measures represent a continuous measurement while strategy-based categorical measurements represent a discrete measurement.

Before assessing the overall diversity of the firm in question, the firm's businesses need to be identified. According to Pitts and Hopkins this is accomplished in one of three ways: (1) a resource approach (as utilized by Rumelt); (2) a market approach; or (3) a product approach. In a resource approach, the focus is on a firm's internal company resources, and researchers "consider a set of activities to constitute a discrete business if the resources involved are separate from those supporting the firm's other activities."[41] A market approach "looks outward from the firm to its market."[42] A product approach "focuses on the product or service that passes between a supplier and its customers, and it considers each product or product type to be a separate business. This approach can be considered to combine elements of the resource and market approaches because a product incorporates some aspects of both dimensions."[43]

Once an approach to the definition of discrete businesses has been settled upon, the overall level of firm diversity can be assessed via business count or strategy measures. Business count measures assess diversity in terms of a count of a firm's businesses. They include numerical count, share of largest business (as utilized by Rumelt), comprehensive indexes, and composite indexes. An example of a comprehensive index is

$$D = 1 - \sum_{i=1}^{h} P_i u_i$$

where P_i is the share of the ith business relative to the firm as a whole, u_i is an assigned weight, and n is the number of the firm's businesses.

Strategy measures are based on the "underlying logic" rather than the number of businesses. These measures are based on either "relatedness" criteria (as employed by Rumelt) or "growth" criteria.

The literature suggests the following considerations in choosing an appropriate measure of diversification. One should consider the relative strengths and weaknesses associated with each measure in terms of data availability and reliability, and the research question at hand. Business count measures are simple, easy to compute, objective, and replicable, but have been criticized because they do not distinguish between related and unrelated diversification. Strategic measures capture this aspect of diversification, but have been criticized because they tend to be subjective and time-consuming.

In an empirical study by Montgomery the two types of measures were compared. Montgomery replicated Rumelt's 1974 work and then compared a product count diversification measure based on standard industry code (SIC) codes to Rumelt's categorical measurement, finding a high degree of correspondence "between the continuous and categorical measures (which) can be interpreted as a 'plus' for SIC-based diversification measures. Such measures have been criticized for their failure to incorporate a broad strategic focus, yet their degree of correspondence with Rumelt's categorical measures suggests that both tap a common underlying continuum." [44]

Palepu utilizes the Jacquemin–Berry entropy measure in his study of firm diversification, asserting that it "enables the researcher to retain the simplicity of the index approach while capturing the essential richness of Rumelt's approach." [45]

The entropy measure of total diversification is defined as:

$$DT = \sum_{i=1}^{h} P_i \ln(1/P_i),$$

where P_i is the share of the ith segment in the total sales of the firm. It measures the number of product segments, the distribution of the firm's total sales across product segments, and the degree of relatedness among the various product segments.

It should be noted that proxies have also been developed in lieu of business count measures. They include size, diversification, and industry diversification.

EMPIRICAL RESULTS

The M-Form Hypothesis and Empirical Results

Williamson's theoretical work in organization theory led him to conclude that the m-form of organization is superior to the functional (u-form) in organizing complex diversified tasks. His formal hypothesis will be restated here:

The organization and operation of the large enterprise along the lines of the M-form (Multidivisional form) favors goal-pursuit and least-cost behavior more nearly associated with the neoclassical profit-maximization hypothesis than does the U-form (functional form) organizational structure.[46]

Many empirical studies have tested this hypothesis and a summary of the literature is presented here. Armour and Teece tested the m-form hypothesis in the petroleum industry, utilizing a sample of twenty-eight firms for the years 1955–1973. Their findings indicated that "characteristics associated with the multidivisional form lead to superior firm performance. That such superior performance is observed only in the 1955–1968 period and not in the 1969–1973 period is consistent with prior arguments made with respect to the diffusion of this organizational form."[47] The m-form hypothesis was also empirically tested in U.K. companies by Steer and Cable, who found "that the internal organization structure of the firms in our sample exerted a statistically significant and large influence on their profitability."[48] Using a classification procedure similar to that of Rumelt and Williamson along with firms in various industries, they modeled firm performance as measured by the price-cost margin as dependent on organizational form. Their methodology was similar to others previously utilized and included regression analysis and the utilization of dummy variables for organizational structure.

Teece also finds support for the m-form hypothesis. What is unique about Teece's study is his employment of a different methodology in testing the performance/structure relationship. In "essence, the methodology involves examining the differential performance between the M-Form 'innovator' in an industry and its principal rival."[49] An advantage of this approach is its ability to control for the effects of market differences, size, product diversity, and industry.

Contrary to previous studies, Harris does not find strong support for the m-form hypothesis. By utilizing two models his findings indicate an approximately equal number of firms experiencing increased profits and decreased profits after adoption of the m-form. He theorizes that "firms which were performing poorly at the time of their adoption of the M-Form organization have improved their performance. This . . . suggests that when the M-Form is part of an adaptive response to poor performance, it provides the type of help contemplated in the M-Form hypothesis."[50]

In still another British study by Hill, which utilized a sample of 144 U.K. companies, support for the m-form hypothesis was found. However, he cautions that "the evidence also suggests that the frequency of occurrence of pure M-form firms as a subset of all multidivisionals may be rather lower than previously thought, and the closeness of the multidivisional/pure M-form link is questioned."[51] Furthermore, "there are clear implications in these results for practitioners. In so far as the pure M-form structure can be judged to be the optimal organizational form for the majority of large UK firms, it appears that there is considerable room for improvement in organizational efficiency."[52]

The question of the "dynamics" involved in the adoption of the m-form is initially addressed by Hoskisson and Galbraith. In order to overcome limitations of earlier studies and explore the dynamics of structural change, they employ time-series intervention analysis. Besides indicating support for the m-form hypothesis, "the results further indicate that managers should consider timing and overall approach when moving to a new organizational form. . . . Structural reorganization appears to be most effective during periods of growth and good times. Structural reorganization may not be good in decline stages and may even augment the problem."[53]

Finally, a novel question is posed with regard to the adoption of the m-form structure by Buhner and Moller. They ask "whether shareholders react to information on multidivisional reorganization in a way which leads to a revision of stock prices. If so, shareholders judge announcements of multidivisional reorganization to have informational content."[54] In other words, do shareholders realize the touted benefits of the m-form, namely, diversification strategies that increase efficiency and profits? Buhner and Moller's findings indicate that they do.

A summary of studies regarding the adoption of the m-form of organizational structure and the m-form hypothesis are summarized in Table 2.1.

Empirical Findings on Diversification Strategy and Performance

In his pioneering study, Rumelt examined the relationship of strategy, structure, and performance in five hundred industrial companies for the period 1949–1969. His findings indicated that related diversification was associated with higher profitability than unrelated diversification. In 1982, he replicated his original study with the following modifications: (1) a change in categories (reduction from the original 9 to 7); and (2) an extension of the sample time period. The findings in this more recent study indicate that the related-constrained firms earned returns on capital that were greater than average. According to Rumelt, the "data show that the high return on capital of the Related Constrained group was primarily an industry effect and that Related Constrained firms perform as would be expected, given the industries in which they participate. . . . However, there remains the question of why Related Constrained firms are concentrated in high-profit industries."[55] The lowest levels of profitability were associated with vertically integrated firms and firms diversifying into unrelated businesses.

In a study by Christensen and Montgomery, which involved a partial replication of Rumelt's work, market structure was introduced as a moderating variable in a test of the diversification/performance relationship. In particular, Christensen and Montgomery assert that "two distinct profits emerge from this work: one for the related constrained, and the other for the unrelated portfolio diversifiers. These firms are distinguished not only by their product linkages and performance levels, but also by the characteristics of the markets in which they operate."[56] Specifically, unrelated firms were found to be located in stag-

Table 2.1
The M-Form Hypothesis

STUDY	SAMPLE	VARIABLES	METHOD	FINDINGS
Armour & Teece (1978)	28 Petroleum Industry firms 1955-1974	ROE, Firm Structure, Extent of Diversification	Regression	Support for the M-Form Hypothesis
Steer & Cable (1978)	82 UK firms 1967-1974	Profitability, Firm structure, Extent of diversification	Regression	Support for the M-Form Hypothesis
Teece (1981)	36 Firms-18 Industries in both before and after adoption year	Rate of Return	Selection of matched pairs, Sign test & Wilcoxian signed rank test	Found in support of the M-Form Hypothesis
Harris (1983)	27 Firms for the years 1954-72	Industry Rate of Return, Rate of Return, Structure	Regression utilizing two models	Conditional support for the M-Form Hypothesis
Hill (1985)	144 Large U.K. firms	Organizational Structure, Return on Sales, Return on Capital, Growth in EPS and Sales	Regression	Generally supportive of M-form Hypothesis for pure M-form firm
Hoskisson & Galbraith (1985)	3 Pairs of firms in 3 industries	ROA, Firm Structure, Type of Organizational Change	Time Series, ARRIMA	Reorganization to M-Form produces a positive effect on performance
Buhner & Moller (1985)	24 Large West German industrials for the period 1965-1975	Profit, Payout Ratios, Risk	Regression	Shareholders appear to be aware of the economic significance of the adoption of the M-form

nant, unprofitable, unconcentrated markets, while the related constrained firms tended to be in profitable, fast-growing markets.

Conflicting findings were indicated by Montgomery in a study of the relationship of diversification, market structure, and performance. By utilizing a different methodology her "results provided no support for the collusive power view of diversification, which sees firms' profitability as a function of their diversification."[57] Actually, it appeared that market share, market profitability, and market growth were determinants of firm profitability.

Two final studies are included in Table 2.2 that summarize empirical findings on the relationship of diversification to firm performance. By utilizing a continuous measure of diversification, coupled with a longitudinal look at performance, Palepu finds that "over time, the profitability growth rate of related diversifiers is significantly greater than that of unrelated diversifiers."[58] Grant, Jammine, and Thomas expanded study in the area to 304 British firms for the years 1972–1984.[59] Unique to their study is the consideration of both product diversity and multinational diversity.

Empirical Studies Regarding Diversification and Risk/Return Tradeoffs

Bettis and Hall extend further the work of Rumelt and others in an attempt to investigate differences in the related and unrelated groups. Unique to this study is the introduction of accounting-determined risk as a moderating variable. Bettis and Hall look at performance differences in related and unrelated strategies, risk differences in diversification, strategies, and the relationship of risk and return to diversification strategy. Their findings indicated "that unrelated firms do not enjoy superior risk-pooling characteristics and that the superior returns attributed by Rumelt to related diversification may be due largely to industry effects."[60]

Looking again at related versus unrelated diversification, Michel and Shaked find empirical evidence that "suggests that firms diversifying in unrelated areas are able to generate statistically superior performance over those businesses that are predominantly related."[61] Relatedness of firms was determined in a manner consistent with that of Rumelt. Individual firm performance was measured in five ways and risk-adjusted performance measures were then regressed on relatedness measures. This study provides us with some initial insight into why firms might pursue an unrelated strategy. Dubofsky and Varadarajan confirmed the above findings and also tested accounting measures of performance. However, conflicting findings were noted when accounting measures of performance replaced market measures. By way of explanation, they suggest that "since market measures reflect the market's perceptions of future earnings and accounting measures reflect a previous year's earnings and a current balance sheet, there might be some discrepancy between the measures if a firm's strategy has a lagged effect."[62]

Table 2.2
Diversification and Firm Performance

STUDY	SAMPLE	DIVERSI-FICATION MEASURE	VARIABLES & METHOD	FINDINGS
Rumelt (1974)	500 Industrials (1949-1969)	Categorical	Performance, Firm Structure. Regression	Dominant constrained most profitable; single & dominant vertical had low sales growth; Acquisitive conglomerate had high growth in sales and earnings
Christensen & Montgomery (1981)	128 Fortune 500 companies 1972-1977	Categorical	Profitability, Firm Structure, Market Structure. Regression	Dominant constrained, Dominant linked & Related Constrained most profitable Vertical integration least profitable Market Structure influenced
Rumelt (1982)	273 Fortune 500 firms 1972-1977	Categorical	ROA, Firm structure. Regression	Related constrained had ROA > average. Dominant vertical and unrelated < average

Table 2.2 (Continued)

STUDY	SAMPLE	DIVERSIFI-CATION MEASURE	VARIABLES & METHOD	FINDINGS
Montgomery (1985)	128 Fortune 500 companies 1972-1977	Continuous Based on SIC codes	ROA, Market share. Regression	SIC based measures of diversity were insignificantly associated with ROA once industry structure and market share were taken into account
Palepu (1985)	30 Firms in the food industry 1973-1979	Entropy Measure	Return on Sales. Regression	No significant cross-sectional relationship. Profitability growth rate for related higher than for unrelated
Grant, Jammine & Thomas (1988)	304 UK firms 1972-1984	Both continuous & categorical	ROA. Static and Dynamic analysis	Diversity and profitability are related up to a point. Differences found in product and multinational diversification

Bettis and Mahajan contribute further to the study of the risk/return relationship and diversification. Building on prior research and utilizing cluster analysis, risk/return profiles for eighty firms are developed. The study indicates that different diversification strategies may in fact result in similar risk/return profiles, and that although related diversification may be a necessary condition for a favorable risk/return profile, it is not a sufficient condition. In their words, "related diversification offers no guarantee for an efficient risk/return performance. Managers should not rely on a related diversification strategy to achieve performance. Much more is needed."[63]

A study by Amit and Livnat extends prior research by examining both accounting and market measures of risk via cluster analysis utilizing a cash flow surrogate for accounting profits: "Although this study showed differences in the risk-return characteristics of firms, we do not and cannot claim that one set of characteristics is better than the others without an explicit knowledge of the risk preferences of shareholders of specific firms."[64] The particular strategy adopted by a firm is formulated by the board of directors or managers who have some control over the organization's resources. If these individuals have large human investments in the firm they may decide to reduce their risk by engaging in unrelated diversification. The range of such diversification may be determined in part by the ownership structure of the firm.

A final recent study deserves attention before considering conclusions and implications for future study of the multidivisional form. Hoskisson supports a contingency view of the relationship between performance and implementation of an m-form structure. The central proposition of such a view is "that implementation of a multidivisional structure creates varying performance levels in firms that employ the different strategic approaches of unrelated diversification, vertical integration, and related diversification."[65] In the case of the unrelated diversifiers who adopted the m-form structure, they were able not only to improve performance but also to reduce risk.

A summary of the aforementioned studies appears in Table 2.3.

This chapter has first examined various theories of the genesis and prevalence of the multidivisional form of organization. Controversy still exists in this area and a robust theory of diversification still forthcoming. Contingency theory as proposed by Hoskisson may be one avenue that merits additional consideration and pursuit. Recently, Hill and Hoskisson questioned an assumption in strategy-structure theory, namely, "that the M-form structure used to manage diversified firms represents a homogeneous set of organizational arrangements."[66] They propose an alternative framework in this vein along with a number of hypotheses begging to be tested.

Various operational definitions and methodologies employed in the analysis of firm structure have also been reviewed here. Again it is evident that more research is needed in the development of proxies and better matching of the

Table 2.3
Diversification, Risk, and Return

STUDY	SAMPLE	VARIABLES	METHOD	FINDINGS
Bettis & Hall (1982)	80 Fortune 500 companies 1973-1977	ROA, Accounting deter-mined risk, 3 catego-ries of firms	Regression Anova	Higher profita-bility due to industry effects. Trade-offs exist in terms of risk and return
Michel & Shaked (1984)	51 Fortune 250 companies 1975-1981	Risk adjusted measures of return, Market measures, Measures of related-ness	Regression	Unrelated diversi-fiers earned higher risk-adjusted equity returns than related
Bettis & Mahajan (1985)	80 firms 1973-1977	Risk, ROA, Categori-cal Diversi-fication measures	Cluster Analysis	Different diversi-fication strategies may result in similar risk/ return profiles. Favorable profile hard to obtain with unrelated
Dubofsky & Varadara-jan (1987)	See Michel & Shaked (1984)	Accounting & Market measures of risk and return, Categori-cal measures of diversity	Regression	Unrelated earned higher risk-adjusted equity returns-no difference in ROA

Table 2.3 (Continued)

STUDY	SAMPLE	VARIABLES	METHOD	FINDINGS
Amit & Livnat (1988)	269 firms 1977-1982	Accounting & market based measures of risk and return, Continuous measures of diversification	Cluster Analysis	High return\ high risk profiles characterize related diversification, while low risk\ low return profiles are associated with unrelated
Hoskisson (1987)	62 firms in 20 industries	Performance, Risk, Strategic measures of diversification	Longitudinal Analysis	Adoption of M-form increases rate of return for unrelated firms, decreases for vertically integrated For related, not significant. Risk usually declined, only significant for unrelated & vertically integrated

research question and the methodology. Methodologies appropriate for testing the dynamic implications of a diversification decision need to be employed.

Finally, conflicting empirical evidence appears to indicate that something is still missing in terms of a moderating variable or variables. Perhaps the answer lies in a more aggressive look at the actors and internal structures (i.e., control structures) in an organization, and the consideration of behavioral factors. Lest we forget, an organization adapts to its external environment, and perhaps more pieces of the puzzle could be found in an examination of political and environmental variables. In the area of related research it is also possible that firm strategy and structure decisions play a role in information content and incentive-oriented research.

NOTES

1. Oliver E. Williamson, *The Economic Institutions of Capitalism* (New York: Free Press, 1985), p. 279.

2. Ibid., p. 281.

3. Neil Fligstein, "The Spread of the Multidivisional Form among Large Firms," *American Sociological Review* 50 (1985): 377–78.

4. Alfred D. Chandler, *Strategy and Structure* (Cambridge, Mass.: MIT, 1962).

5. Ibid., p. 14.

6. See Fligstein, "Spread of the Multidivisional Form among Large Firms," p. 378, for a discussion.

7. Chandler, *Strategy and Structure,* p. 13.

8. Ibid., p. 382.

9. Williamson, *Economic Institutions of Capitalism.*

10. Ibid., p. 280.

11. Oliver E. Williamson, *Corporate Control and Business Behavior* (Englewood Cliffs, N.J.: Prentice-Hall, 1970), p. 20.

12. Williamson, *Economic Institutions of Capitalism,* p. 30.

13. Ibid., pp. 280–81.

14. Williamson, *Corporate Control and Business Behavior,* p. 134.

15. Donald Palmer et al., "The Economics and Politics of Structure: The Multidivisional Form and the Large U.S. Corporation," *Administrative Science Quarterly* 32 (1987): 31.

16. For a discussion, see Michael Hannan and John Freeman, "Structural Inertia and Organizational Change," *American Sociological Review* 49 (1984): 149–64.

17. Fligstein, "Spread of the Multidivisional Form among Large Firms," p. 379.

18. Ibid., p. 380.

19. Palmer et al., "Economics and Politics of Structure," p. 29.

20. Gerald R. Salancik and Jeffrey Pfeffer, "Effects of Ownership and Performance on Executive Tenure in U.S. Corporations," *Academy of Management Journal* 23 (1980): 655.

21. Palmer, et al., "Economics and Politics of Structure," p. 29.

22. Fligstein, "Spread of the Multidivisional Form among Large Firms," p. 380.

23. Ibid., p. 388.

24. Ibid.

25. Ibid.

26. Ibid., p. 389.

27. David J. Teece, "Towards an Economic Theory of the Multiproduct Firm," *Journal of Economic Behavior and Organizations* 3 (1982): 61.

28. Ibid., p. 47.

29. Palmer et al., "Economics and Politics of Structure," p. 42.

30. Ibid., p. 43.

31. Richard P. Rumelt, "Diversification Strategy and Profitability," *Strategic Management Journal* 3 (1982): 359.

32. Richard P. Rumelt, *Strategy, Structure, and Economic Performance* (Cambridge, Mass.: Harvard University Press, 1974), p. 69.

33. Ibid.

34. Ibid., p. 150.

35. Ibid., p. 152.

36. Allen Michel and Israel Shaked, "Does Business Diversification Affect Performance?" *Financial Management* (Winter 1984): 18.

37. Ibid., p. 19.

38. Charles W. L. Hill and Robert E. Hoskisson, "Strategy and Structure in the Multiproduct Firm," *Academy of Management Review* 12/2 (1987): 331.

39. Ibid., pp. 332–33.

40. Rumelt, *Strategy, Structure, and Economic Performance,* p. 9.

41. Robert A. Pitts and H. Donald Hopkins, "Firm Diversity: Conceptualization and Management," *Academy of Management Review* 74 (1982): 621.

42. Ibid.

43. Ibid.

44. Cynthia A. Montgomery, "The Measurement of Firm Diversification: Some New Empirical Evidence," *Academy of Management Journal* 25/2 (1982): 305.

45. Krishna Palepu, "Diversification Strategy, Profit Performance and the Entropy Measure," *Strategic Management Journal* 6 (1985): 244.

46. Williamson, *Corporate Control and Business Behavior,* p. 134.

47. Henry Ogden Armour and David J. Teece, "Organizational Structure and Economic Performance: A Test of the Multidivisional Hypothesis," *Bell Journal of Economics* 9 (1978): 119.

48. Peter Steer and John Cable, "Internal Organization and Profit: An Empirical Analysis of Large U.K. Companies," *Journal of Industrial Economics* 27 (1978): 28.

49. David J. Teece, "Internal Organization and Economic Performance: An Empirical Analysis of the Profitability of Principal Firms," *Journal of Industrial Economics* 30 (1981): 173.

50. Barry C. Harris, *Organization, The Effect on Large Corporations* (Ann Arbor, Mich.: UMI Research Press, 1983), p. 55.

51. Charles W. L. Hill, "Internal Organization and Enterprise Performance: Some U.K. Evidence," *Managerial and Decision Economics* 6/4 (1985): 210.

52. Ibid., pp. 215–216.

53. Robert E. Hoskisson and Craig S. Galbraith, "The Effect of Quantum versus Incremental M-Form Reorganization on Performance: A Time-Series Exploration of Intervention Dynamics," *Journal of Management Studies* 11/3 (1985): 69.

54. R. Buhner and P. Moller, "The Information Content of Corporate Disclosures of Divisionalization Decisions," *Journal of Management Studies* 22/3 (1985): 310.

55. Rumelt, "Diversification Strategy and Profitability," p. 368.

56. H. Kurt Christensen and Cynthia A. Montgomery, "Corporate Economic Performance: Diversification Strategy vs. Market Structure," *Strategic Management Journal* 2 (1981): 338.

57. Cynthia Montgomery, "Product-Market Diversification and Market Power," *Academy of Management Journal* 28/4 (1985): 793.

58. Palepu, "Diversification Strategy, Profit Performance and the Entropy Measure," p. 250.

59. Robert M. Grant, Azar P. Jammine, and Howard Thomas, "Diversity, Diversification, and Profitability among British Manufacturing Companies, 1972–84," *Academy of Management Journal* 31/4 (1988): 771–801.

60. Richard A. Bettis and William K. Hall, "Diversification Strategy, Accounting Determined Risk, and Accounting Determined Return," *Academy of Management Journal* 25/2 (1982): 254.

61. Michel and Shaked, "Does Business Diversification Affect Performance?" p. 24.

62. Paulette Dubofsky and P. "Rajan" Varadarajan, "Diversification and Measures of Performance: Additional Empirical Evidence," *Academy of Management Journal* 30/3 (1987): 606.

63. Richard A. Bettis and Vijay Mahajan, "Risk/Return Performance of Diversified Firms," *Management Science* 31/7 (1985): 796.

64. Raphael Amit and Joshua Livnat, "Diversification and the Risk-Return Trade-Off," *Academy of Management Journal* 31/1 (1988): 161.

65. Robert E. Hoskisson, "Multidivisional Structure and Performance: The Contingency of Diversification Strategy," *Academy of Management Journal* 30/4 (1987): 638.

66. Hill and Hoskisson, "Strategy and Structure in the Multiproduct Firm," p. 331.

REFERENCES

Amit, Raphael and Joshua Livnat. 1988. Diversification and the risk-return trade-off. *Academy of Management Journal* 31 (1): 154–166.

Armour, Henry Ogden and David J. Teece. 1978. Organizational structure and economic performance: A test of the multidivisional hypothesis. *Bell Journal of Economics* 9: 106–122.

Bettis, Richard A. and William K. Hall. 1982. Diversification strategy, accounting determined risk, and accounting determined return. *Academy of Management Journal* 25 (2): 254–264.

Bettis, Richard A. and Vijay Mahajan. 1985. Risk/return performance of diversified firms. *Management Science* 31 (7): 785–799.

Buhner, R. and P. Moller. 1985. The information content of corporate disclosures of divisionalization decisions. *Journal of Management Studies* 22 (3): 309–326.

Christensen, H. Kurt and Cynthia A. Montgomery. 1981. Corporate economic performance: Diversification strategy vs. market structure. *Strategic Management Journal* 2: 327–343.

Dubofsky, Paulette and P. "Rajan" Varadarajan. 1987. Diversification and measures of performance: Additional empirical evidence. *Academy of Management Journal* 30 (3): 597–608.

Grant, Robert M., Azar P. Jammine, and Howard Thomas. 1988. Diversity, diversification, and profitability among British manufacturing companies, 1972–84. *Academy of Management Journal* 31 (4): 771–801.

Harris, Barry C. 1983. *Organization, The Effect on Large Corporations.* Ann Arbor, Mich.: UMI Research Press.

Hill, Charles W. L. 1985. Internal organization and enterprise performance: Some U.K. evidence. *Managerial and Decision Economics* 6 (4): 210–214.

Hoskisson, Robert E. 1987. Multidivisional structure and performance: The contingency of diversification strategy. *Academy of Management Journal* 30 (4): 625–644.

Hoskisson, Robert E. and Craig S. Galbraith. 1985. The effect of quantum versus incremental M-form reorganization on performance: A time-series exploration of intervention dynamics. *Journal of Management* 11 (3): 55–70.

Michel, Allen and Israel Shaked. 1984. Does business diversification affect performance? *Financial Management* (Winter): 18–25.

Montgomery, Cynthia. 1985. Product-market diversification and market power. *Academy of Management Journal* 28 (4): 789–798.

Palepu, Krishna. 1985. Diversification strategy, profit performance and the entropy measure. *Strategic Management Journal* 6:239–255.

Rumelt, Richard P. 1982. Diversification strategy and profitability. *Strategic Management Journal* 3: 359–369.

————. 1974. *Strategy, Structure, and Economic Performance.* Cambridge, Mass.: Harvard University Press.

Steer, Peter and John Cable. 1978. Internal organization and profit: An empirical analysis of large U.K. companies. *Journal of Industrial Economics* 27: 13–30.

Teece, David J. 1982. Towards an economic theory of the multiproduct firm. *Journal of Economic Behavior* 3: 39–63.

THE OWNERSHIP STRUCTURE THESIS

Berle and Means advance the thesis that ownership and control have been separated in the case of the large corporation, and that this separation has certain implications for the conduct of the large firm. "If the individual is protected in the right both to use his property as he sees fit and to receive the full fruits of its use, his desire for personal gain, for profits, can be relied upon as an effective incentive to his efficient use of any industrial property he may possess."[1] In the large modern corporation, this assumption no longer holds. It is no longer the individual (owner) who uses wealth, but rather corporate executives who control resources and are in a position to use them efficiently to produce profits. These managers or executives may not necessarily be the owners of such resources who are entitled to those profits.

In a large corporation, there are generally so many stockholders that no one individual or group may own a significant fraction of the outstanding voting stock; corporate officers, including the CEO, own a very small fraction of the outstanding stock; and the interests of management and stockholders (owners) diverge. The diffusion of stock ownership, by modifying the link between ownership and control, may be viewed as undermining the role of profit maximization as a guide to resource allocation. In other words, diffusion of ownership may render the owners powerless to control the actions of management.

One much debated ramification of the separation of ownership and control in the large firm is its effect upon firm performance. One school of thought argues that the distribution of ownership has important implications for the efficiency and strategic development of the firm, suggesting in particular that when an executive's pay is positively related to firm size, the firms themselves will be operated to maximize sales rather than profits. Others argue the irrelevance of the separation of ownership and control, asserting that "the firm is disciplined by competition from other firms, which forces the evolution of devices for effectively monitoring the performance of the entire team and of its individual members. In addition, individual participants in the firm, and in particular its managers, face both the discipline and opportunities provided by the markets for their services."[2]

Another ramification of the separation of ownership and control in the large firm is found in certain observed managerial practices such as "income smoothing," defined as "managers' attempt to 'manipulate' income numbers so as to impart to the resulting series a 'desirable' and 'smooth' trend."[3] According to E. Daniel Smith, the accounting profession "has provided management one means by which they may generate a relatively smooth income stream. The wide variety of reporting alternatives considered to be acceptable representations of the events of any particular period provides management with a range of possible profit figures for any one period."[4] Furthermore, Schiff argues that "if there is a conflict between the managers' and owners' interests in corporations with diffuse ownership, the opportunity to choose the accounting method gives an important advantage to the manager."[5]

Finally, if there is in fact a difference between the interests of owners and managers or executives, "it follows logically that with great separation of control, the making of policies and decisions will not adequately reflect the interests of owners. . . . Type of control could be a key determinant of the pay levels of chief executives."[6] Allen argues that "the fact that chief executive officers often possess the power to influence their own levels of compensation has been ignored."[7] The business press has even speculated that CEOs tend to overcompensate themselves because of the unchallenged power that they enjoy within an organization. While power or control is derived from many sources, one cannot deny that the control of a significant block of outstanding stock enhances control.

OWNERSHIP STRUCTURE AND FIRM PERFORMANCE

Theories Underlying the Relativity of Ownership Structure

Dispersion of Ownership Interests Theory

Berle and Means advance the thesis that ownership and control have been separated in the case of the large corporation, and that this separation has implications for the conduct of the firm. "If an individual has the right to use his property as he sees fit and receives the full fruits of it, his desire for gain or profit provides an effective incentive to use his industrial property efficiently."[8] In a quasi-public corporation, the above assumption no longer holds. Dispersion of ownership renders the owners powerless to control the actions of management. Since the interest of owners and managers does not naturally coincide, resources are not used entirely in pursuit of shareholder wealth.

Theoretically, the insights of Berle and Means have given rise to competing hypotheses that explore the role of management ownership of stock in firm performance and risk (see Figure 3.1).

Figure 3.1
Theorized Relationships of Ownership Structure and Firm Performance

DISPERSION OF OWNERSHIP INTERESTS THEORY

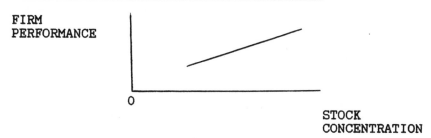

CONVERGENCE-OF-INTERESTS HYPOTHESIS

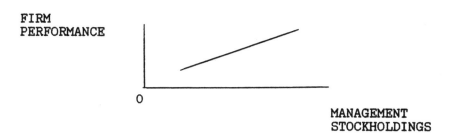

ENTRENCHMENT HYPOTHESIS

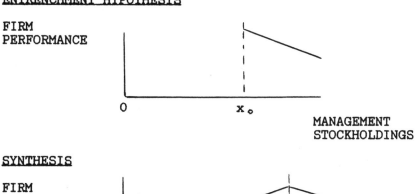

SYNTHESIS

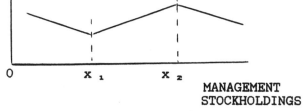

The Convergence-of-Interests Hypothesis

The convergence-of-interests hypothesis has its theoretical roots in agency theory, the concern of which is the alignment of the interests of principals (owners) and agents (managers).[9] When managers hold little equity in the firm and there exists diffusion of ownership among principals, monitoring and enforcement of optimal actions (those enhancing shareholder wealth) become costly and difficult, and the managers are predisposed to shirk, indulge in perquisites, and in general undermine the interests of owners. When the stakes of managers in the organization are raised, managers are made to bear a larger share of the cost of their nonvalue-maximizing decisions.

By offering incentives to participate in decisions leading to profit-maximizing behavior, the interests of management and owners are better aligned. Therefore, the convergence-of-interests hypothesis predicts a uniformly positive relationship between management stockholdings and firm performance (see figure 3.1).

The Entrenchment Hypothesis

The entrenchment hypothesis points out that there are offsetting costs to significant management stock ownership.[10] When managers own a small stake, the forces of the market may still force them toward value maximization (this is consistent with the convergence-of-interests hypothesis). However, when managers control a substantial fraction, they may have enough voting power or influence to guarantee employment with the firm, and therefore may indulge in their preference for nonvalue-maximizing behavior. This hypothesis predicts that there may be a negative relationship between management stockholdings and firm performance for some high range of management stockholding (see Figure 3.1).

Synthesis

According to the convergence-of-interests hypothesis, firm performance increases as management ownership increases. Berle and Means argue that the dispersion of shareholders' ownership allows managers holding little equity in the firm to forego value (wealth) maximization and use corporate assets to benefit themselves rather than the shareholders.[11] Jensen and Meckling contend instead that the costs of deviation from value maximization decline as managers' stakes in the firm rises, as managers are less likely to squander corporate wealth when they have to pay a larger share of the costs.[12]

According to the entrenchment hypothesis, firm performance does not rise with management ownership. Demsetz[13] and Fama and Jensen[14] have pointed out the offsetting costs associated with higher management stockholdings. If managers have a small stockholding, they will work toward value maximization as a result of factors including market discipline (e.g., in the managerial labor market[15] and the product market[16]) and the market for corporate control.[17] If managers hold a larger proportion of a firm's stock, however, giving them enough voting power to guarantee their jobs, they may opt for nonvalue-maximizing behavior.

What the two hypotheses imply in conjunction with recent empirical findings is that firm performance will be positively related to lower ranges of management ownership and negatively related to higher ranges of management ownership. In other words, a nonmonotonic relationship is implied (see Figure 3.1).[18]

Empirical Research on the Relationship of Ownership Structure to Firm Performance

Studies on the relationship of ownership structure to firm performance are summarized in Table 3.1. The studies differ in three main aspects: definition of the ownership structure variable(s); nature of the firm performance variables; and methodology (in particular, whether or not they were looking at a linear or nonlinear relationship).

In order to operationalize the concept of control, studies have varied in their definition of ownership structure variables. The most common approach involves classifying a firm as either manager- or owner-controlled based upon an arbitrary criterion such as 5 percent of the corporation's voting stock in the hands of a particular group.[19] Other studies have relied upon categorical classifications of control based on decision rules.[20] Still others have relied upon a one-time-only 1980 data set assembled by the Corporate Data Exchange in order to develop continuous measures of ownership structure. Demsetz and Lehn, for example, utilize separate regression models for each of three measures of stock concentration in order to estimate the linear cross-sectional relationship between a firm's average return on equity and ownership structure for 511 large firms.[21] The three measures of stock ownership utilized were: percent owned by the five largest stockholders; percent owned by the twenty largest stockholders; and the sum of the squared percentage holding of each stockholder in the firm. Drawing on this same data base, Hill and Snell developed continuous measures of both stock concentration and management stockholdings.[22] Finally, in a recent study by Belkaoui and Pavlik, continuous measurements of both stock concentration and manager stockholdings were developed from information reported in the proxy statements for 228 firms for the year 1987.[23]

Studies in this area have also varied in the way firm performance is measured and in some studies differences in risk are also considered.[24] Performance measures include both accounting (rates of return) and market (market capitalization) measures. Finally, although most previous studies assumed and tested for a linear relationship, a few recent studies test for a nonlinear relationship.[25]

Theory suggests that owner-controlled firms will outperform manager-controlled firms due to the nonprofit-maximizing behavior of managers. However, "findings . . . are mixed and consequently do not lead to a consensus on the effect of a separation of ownership from control on measures of firm performance and risk."[26] While the reason for the mixed results has been attributed

Table 3.1
Ownership Structure and Firm Performance

STUDY	SAMPLE	VARIABLES	MEASUREMENT OF OWNERSHIP STRUCTURE	METHODOLOGY	FINDINGS
Kamerschen (1968)	200 large non-financial corpora-tions for 1963	Rate of Return, Concentra-tion, Growth, Sales, Barriers to entry, Assets, Invested capital	0-1 dummy variable	Regression	No significant control effect on profit rates
Monsen Chiu Cooley (1968)	36 firms of each control type-owner or manager	Net income, Net worth, Sales/ Assets, NI/Assets, NI/Sales, LT Debt/ Total Capitali-zation, Industry, Size	Dichotomous either owner controlled or manager controlled	Three-way analysis of covariance	Owner controlled group of firms out-performed manager controlled firms
Boudreaux (1973)	72 large manufactu-ring firms (1952-1963)	Return on Equity, STD, Deviation of Return on Equity, Size, Industry	Either owner or manager controlled	Analysis of Covariance	Owner controlled group had higher rates of return and more variable returns than manager controlled firms
Palmer (1973)	500 large companies (1961-1965) and (1966-1969)	Rate of return on on Net Worth, Monopoly Power, Firm Size	3 category classification for control	Analysis of Covariance	Owner controlled firms with high degree of monopoly power had higher returns

Table 3.1 (Continued)

STUDY	SAMPLE	VARIABLES	MEASUREMENT OF OWNERSHIP STRUCTURE	METHODOLOGY	FINDINGS
Salancik Pfeffer (1980)	84 large firms (1963-1973)	Tenure, Return on Common Stock, Total Assets, Average Profit	3 category classification for control	Regression	Ownership mediates the relationship between tenure and performance Tenure was positively related to performance in manager controlled firms, and slightly negative for owner controlled
Amihud Kamin Ronen (1983)	56 firms of Boudreaux sample	Market based risk measures, operating income, operating expenses	Owner or Manager controlled	Regression	Risk measures are higher for owner controlled firms
Demsetz Lehn (1985)	511 firms (1980)	Ownership concentration, Rate of return, Total Assets, Stability of stock returns, Firm dummy variables	Continuous measure of stock concentration	Regression	No significant relationship between ownership concentration and profit rates
Dann Deangelo (1988)	33 firms that announced ownership restructuring in response to hostile takeover bid (1969-1983)	shareholder wealth	n/a	Event-study	Shareholder wealth declines on the average as managers respond to takeovers with defensive changes in ownership structure

Table 3.1 (Continued)

STUDY	SAMPLE	VARIABLES	MEASUREMENT OF OWNERSHIP STRUCTURE	METHODOLOGY	FINDINGS
Holderness Sheehan (1988)	114 firms with majority stockholders (1978-1984)	Executive compensation, Investment policy, Tobin´s Q, Rate of return.	50% majority holder	Regression	Differences in performance between majority-held and diffusely held firms small
Morck Shleifer Vishny (1988)	249 Fortune 500 firms 1980	Tobin´s Q Net cash flows/ replacement cost of capital stock, Industry	Four categories of board ownership	Regression	Positive association between board holdings and performance up to a point
Hill Snell (1989)	Cross-sectional 122 firms	Diversification, R&D, Productivity	Continuous measures of Stock Concentration and Management Stockholding	Path Analysis	Ownership structure affects productivity directly and indirectly
Smith (1989)	58 MBO firms	Absolute and relative performance measures	% stock owned by 1) officers 2) outside directors and 3) other major holders	Regression	Substantial increases in profitability following MBO
Kole (1990)	371 firms (1980)	Market Value/ Replacement Cost, Profit, Avg. Profit	3 categories of Board ownership- $\leq$ 5%, 5-25%, and >25%	Piecewise-Linear regression	Sensitivity of firm performance to board ownership is non-uniform. Past firm firm performance determines ownership
Belkaoui Pavlik (1990)	228 firms (1987)	Profit Market Capitalization	2 Continuous measures- Stock Concentration & Management Stockholdings	Piecewise-Linear Regression	Ownership structure affects performance Relationship is nonlinear

to the problems with data found by researchers when attempting to construct either meaningful measures of the distribution of stock ownership[27] or measures of performance,[28] Morck, Schleifer, and Vishny argue that theory suggests a nonmonotonic relationship between management ownership and the market valuation of the firm.[29] They estimate the cross-sectional relationship between stock ownership by the board of directors and corporate performance in 1980 for a sample of 249 firms in the Fortune 500. Two measures of corporate performance are used: Tobin's Q and the ratio of net cash flows to the replacement cost of capital stock.

Unlike Demsetz and Lehn,[30] they relax the assumption of a linear relation between performance and stock ownership, and propose a nonmonotonic relationship instead. They test for different average performance (i.e., regression model intercept) for each of the following categories of board holdings: (1) less than 0.2 percent; (2) between 0.2 and 5 percent; (3) between 5 and 20 percent; and (4) greater than 20 percent. They find evidence of a nonmonotonic relationship. Tobin's Q increases, then declines, and finally rises slightly as ownership by the board of directors rises.

A recent study by Belkaoui and Pavlik[31] expands the Morck, Schleifer, and Vishny study by proposing two different measures of ownership structure, namely, stock concentration and management stockholdings, and two measures of performance for a recent sample of large U.S. firms. Their findings indicate a significant nonmonotonic relationship between profit and market capitalization on the one hand and management stockholdings and stock concentration on the other. More explicitly, both profit and market capitalization decline as management stockholdings rise from 0 to 5 percent, increase as management stockholdings rise further to 25 percent, and then decline as management stockholdings rise above 25 percent. The interpretation is compatible with: (1) a dispersion of ownership and nonvalue-maximizing behavior by management for less than 5 percent ownership; (2) a convergence of interests between managers and shareholders between 5 and 25 percent ownership; and (3) an entrenchment of the management team as their stakes exceed 25 percent. Similarly, both profit and market capitalization decline as stock concentration increases from 0 to 25 percent, then rise as the stock concentration exceeds 25 percent. The interpretation is compatible with the need for a large stock concentration before stockholders can influence management decisions toward value-maximizing behavior.

OWNERSHIP STRUCTURE AND ACCOUNTING PRINCIPLE CHOICE

The Nature of Income Smoothing

Income smoothing is the deliberate normalization of income numbers in order to reach a desired trend or level. As far back as 1953, Hepworth noted "some of the accounting techniques which may be applied to affect the assignment of net income to successive accounting periods . . . for smoothing or leveling the amplitude of periodic net income fluctuations.''[32] What followed were arguments that corporate managers may be motivated to smooth their own income (or security), with the assumption that stability in income and rate of growth will be preferred over higher average income streams with greater variability.[33] The best definition of income smoothing is provided by Beidleman:

Smoothing of reported earnings may be defined as the intentional dampening of fluctuation about some level of earnings that is currently considered to be normal for a firm. In this sense smoothing represents an attempt on the part of the firm's management to reduce abnormal variations in earnings to the extent allowed under sound accounting and management principles.[34]

The Motivations for Smoothing

Hepworth claims that motivations for smoothing include the improvements of relations with creditors, investors, and workers as well as dampening of business cycles through psychological processes.[35] Gordon proposes that: (1) the criterion corporate management uses in selecting accounting principles is to maximize its utility or welfare; (2) this same utility is a function of job security, the level and rate of growth of salary, and the level and growth rate of the firm's size; (3) satisfaction of stockholders with the corporation's performance enhances the status and rewards of managers; and (4) this same satisfaction depends on the rate of growth and stability of the firm's income.[36] These propositions culminate in the need to smooth as explained in the following theorem:

Given that the above four propositions are accepted or found to be true, it follows that a management should within the limits of its power, i.e., the latitude allowed by accounting rules, (1) smooth reported income, and (2) smooth the rate of growth in income. By smooth the rate of growth in income we mean the following: if the rate of growth in income is high, accounting practices which reduce it should be adopted and vice versa.[37]

Beidleman considers two reasons for management to smooth reported earnings.[38] The first argument rests on the assumption that a stable earnings stream is capable of supporting a higher level of dividends than a more variable earnings stream, and has a favorable effect on the value of the firm's shares as overall riskiness of the firm is reduced. ''To the extent that the observed variability about a trend of reported earnings influences investors' subjective expectations for possible outcomes of future earnings and dividends, management might be able favorably to influence the value of the firm's shares by smoothing earnings.''[39]

The second argument attributes to smoothing the ability to counter the cyclical nature of reported earnings and thereby reduce the correlation of a firm's expected returns with returns on the market portfolio. ''To the degree that auto-normalization of earnings is successful and that the reduced covariance of returns with the market is recognized by investors and incorporated into their valuation processes, smoothing will have added beneficial effects on share values."[40] This results from the need felt by management to neutralize environmental uncertainty and damper the wide fluctuations in the operating performance of the firm subject to an intermittent cycle of good and bad times. To do so management may resort to organizational slack behavior,[41] budgetary slack behavior,[42] or risk-avoiding behavior.[43] Each of these behaviors necessitates decisions affecting the incurrence and/or allocation of discretionary expenses (costs) that result in income smoothing.

In addition to behaviors intended to neutralize environmental uncertainty, it is also possible to identify organizational characterizations that differentiate among different firms in their extent of smoothing. Kamin and Ronen examine the effects of the separation of ownership and control on income smoothing under the hypothesis that management-controlled firms are more likely to be engaged in smoothing as a manifestation of managerial discretion and budgetary slack.[44] Their results confirm that a majority of firms behave as if they were smoothers and a particularly strong majority is included among management-controlled firms with high barriers to entry.

Management is assumed to circumvent some of the constraints of generally accepted accounting principles by attempting to smooth income numbers so as to convey their expectations of future cash flows, enhancing in the process the apparent reliability of prediction based on the observed smoothed series of numbers.[45] Three constraints are presumed to lead managers to smooth: "(a) the competitive market mechanisms which reduce the options available to management; (b) the management compensation scheme which is linked directly to the firm performance; and (c) the threat of manager displacement."[46]

This smoothing is not limited to upper-level management and external accounting; it is also presumed to be used by lower-level management and internal accounting in the form of organizational slack and slack budgeting.[47] Recently the terminology has changed from income smoothing to earnings management. Earnings management is shown to be motivated by management's desire to increase annual compensation[48] and influence proxy contests,[49] and the likelihood of foreign trade regulation.[50]

The Dimensions of Smoothing

The dimensions of smoothing are basically the means used to accomplish the smoothing of income numbers. Dascher and Malcolm distinguish between real smoothing and artificial smoothing as follows: "Real smoothing refers to an actual transaction that is undertaken or not undertaken on the basis of its smoothing effect on income, whereas artificial smoothing refers to accounting procedures which are implemented to shift costs and/or revenues from one period to another."[51] These types of smoothing may be indistinguishable. For

example, the amount of reported expenses may be higher or lower than previous periods because of either deliberate actions on the level of expenses (real
smoothing) or the reporting methods (artificial smoothing). For both types an
operational test is proposed to fit a curve to a steam of income calculated two
ways: excluding a possible manipulative variable and including it. "If the variation of the observations around the curve is smaller in the latter case, income
smoothing has been the consequence of transactions in the account."[52]

Copeland defines artificial smoothing as follows: "Income smoothing involves the repetitive selection of accounting measurement or reporting rules in
a particular pattern, the effect of which is to report the stream of income with
a smaller variation from trend than would otherwise have appeared."[53]

Besides real and artificial smoothing, other dimensions of smoothing are considered in the literature. A popular classification adds a third smoothing dimension, namely, classificatory smoothing. Barnea, Ronen, and Sadan distinguish
among three smoothing dimensions:

1. *Smoothing through an event's occurrence and/or recognition.* Management can time
   actual transactions so that their effects on reported income would tend to dampen its
   variation over time. Mostly, the planned timing of an event's occurrences (e.g.,
   research and development) would be a function of the accounting rules governing
   the accounting regulation of the event.

2. *Smoothing through allocation over time.* Given the occurrence and recognition of an
   event, management has more discretionary control over the determination of the
   periods to be affected by the event's quantification.

3. *Smoothing through classification (hence classificatory smoothing).* When income
   statement statistics other than net income (net of all revenues and expenses) are the
   object of smoothing, management can classify intraincome statement items to reduce
   variations over time in that statistic.[54]

Basically real smoothing corresponds to the smoothing through an event's occurrence and/or recognition, while artificial smoothing corresponds to the
smoothing through the allocation over time.

The Focus of Smoothing

The focus of smoothing is the smoothing variable that management chooses
to change in order to reach a desired objective. They can choose net income,
ordinary income, or per share figures or ratios because of the belief of investors' interests in those variables. White argues for the choice of earnings per
share as an "appropriate surrogate for reported performance because of the
heavy emphasis placed on this measure in annual report presentation and traditional security analysis."[55]

Copeland and Licastro choose as the focus of smoothing the dividends received from unconsolidated subsidiaries reported by the parent at cost.[56] They

argue for their choice as follows: "The dividend-income variable was selected because it is an annually recurring item, and thus more open to management's manipulation if it wished to do so. Thus management could conceivably smooth with dividend income each period, rather than only in the periods when a particular decision situation availed itself."[57]

Income before and after extraordinary items may be also smoothed by the classification of an item as either extraordinary or ordinary, especially where the classification is subject to some managerial discretion. As stated by Barnea, Ronen, and Sadan:

Nonrecurring items could, within bounds, be classified as ordinary or extraordinary. Thus, if management wishes to impart a smoother appearance to the reported stream of "ordinary income before extraordinary items," it can use whatever discretion it has in the classification of nonrecurring items to achieve its objective. This is particularly true prior to Opinion 30 . . . because Opinion 9 . . . did leave management more flexibility in classifying nonrecurring items as either ordinary or extraordinary.[58]

The exhaustive list of smoothing variables cannot be compiled as long as there are various built-in flexibilities in the generally accepted accounting principles. It seems that each new Financial Accounting Standards Board (FASB) standard includes built-in flexibility to allow in general the potential for management to fit their particular circumstances to the situation. Examples include FASB #13 on accounting for leases, which may allow management to structure leasing contracts so as to produce either an expensing or a capitalization treatment. Another example is FASB #52, where management may produce a definition of functional currency that favors either a temporal method or a current rate method treatment.

There is no clear consensus on what a good smoothing variable is. Copeland considers a perfect smoothing variable one that meets the following standards:

• Its use must not commit the firm to any particular future action.
• It should rest on professional judgment and be consistent with generally accepted accounting principles.
• It results in material shifts relative to year-to-year differences in income.
• It is merely a reclassification of internal account balances rather than a real transaction with other parties.
• Its use over consecutive periods of time can be in conjunction with other practices.[59]

Beidleman suggests the following two criteria as being necessary for an effective smoothing technique:

1. It must permit management to reduce the variability in reported earnings as it strives to achieve its long-run earnings (growth) objective.
2. Once used, it should not commit the firm to any particular future action.[60]

Stratification in the Dual Economy and Income Smoothing

Theories of dual economy suggest that these sectoral differences have important implications for the opportunity structures and environments faced by individual firms. Firms in the periphery sector face a more restricted opportunity structure and a higher degree of environmental uncertainty than firms in the core sector.

Environmental uncertainty is more evident with regard to the market for labor. The core sector is characterized by high productivity, nonpoverty wages, and employment stability, while the periphery sector is characterized by relatively low average and marginal productivity, low wages, and employment instability. The core sector uses its market power and high degree of profitability to hire and train the best workers and maintain nonpoverty wage levels without seriously eroding their profit margin. Beck, Horan, and Tolbert examined the importance of industrial sectors as hypothesized by the dual economy literature on the process of earnings determination and found substantively and statistically significant differences in the labor force composition and economic status between core and periphery industrial sectors.[61] A direct result of this situation is that turnover in the core sector is likely to be more expensive and less attractive than in the periphery sector. As stated by Harrison:

Secondary (periphery) employers have several reasons for placing a low value on turnover, in sharp contrast to their fellows in the primary market. They can, as a rule, neither afford nor do their technologies require them to invest heavily in "specific training." Instead, they tend to rely on the "general training" (e.g., literacy, basic arithmetic) provided socially. With minimal investment in their current labor force, and given the ready availability of substitute labor outside the firm, such employers are at the very least indifferent to the rate of turnover.[62]

Given this evidence on the differences in labor composition, economic status of employees, low turnover, higher wages, and unionized labor force, the firms in the core industry face less uncertainty in their labor management than firms in the periphery industry. Firms in the periphery industry have more opportunity and more predisposition to smooth both their operating flows (for example, through their labor management) and reported income measures, than firms in the core sector. In other words, the two economic sectors rely on their differential ability to maximize profits through the structuring of their labor processes.[63]

A Test for Smoothing

The following test was utilized in studies of income smoothing by Kamin and Ronen[64] and Belkaoui and Picur.[65] It consists of observing the behavior of the following smoothing variables: (1) operating expenses (OPEX) not included in cost of sales; (2) ordinary expenses (OREX); (3) operating expenses plus ordinary expenses (OPEX + OREX); (4) operating income (OP); and (5) ordinary income (OR).

It is assumed that management knows the future streams of inflows and outflows and their time distinction, and has determined the normal trend of OP or OR. To determine their normal trend, two expectation models have been used: a time trend model and a market trend model.

Insofar as the time trend model, two models have been utilized. First, the series of smoothed variables OP and OR, and of smoothing variables OPEX, OREX, and OPEX + OREX, were detrended in a time-series regression over a maximum span of twenty years (1958–1977) as per equation (1):

$$Y_{ijt} = a_{ij} + \beta'_{ijt} + \epsilon_{ijt}, \ i = 1,2,3,4,5, \ t = 1958, \ . \ . \ . \ 1977, \tag{1}$$

where $i = 1$ for OP, $i = 2$ for OR, $i = 3$ for OPEX, $i = 4$ for OREX, and $i = 5$ for OPEX + OREX, and Y_{ijt} = observed OP,OR,OPEX,OREX,OPEX + OREX for firm j in year t.

Second, the first differences in OPEX, OREX, and OPEX + OREX were detrended in a time regression as per equation (2):

$$\Delta Y_{ijt} = \sigma'_{ij} + \theta'_{ijt}, \ i = 1,2,3, \ t = 1958 \ . \ . \ . \ 1977, \tag{2}$$

where $i = 1$ for OPEX, 2 for OREX, and 3 for OPEX + OREX.

With regard to the market trend model, the first differences in OP, OR, OREX, OPEX, and OPEX + OREX were regressed on a macroindex of first differences measured respectively as the mean observed first differences of OP, OR, OPEX, OREX, and OPEX + OREX as per equation (3):

$$\Delta Y_{ijt} = a'_{ij} + \beta'_{ij} M_{it} + \epsilon'_{ijt}, \ i = 1,2,3,4,5, \ t = 1958, \ . \ . \ . \ 1977, \tag{3}$$

where $i = 1$ for OP, 2 for OR, 3 for OPEX, 4 for OREX, and 5 for OPEX + OREX, M_{it} = sample mean index of OP, OR, OPEX, OREX, and OPEX + OREX where $M_{it} = \dfrac{1}{N} \sum\limits_{i=1}^{N} \Delta Y_{ijt}$, N being the sample size.

Empirical Research

Empirical research on the effect of ownership structure on the choice of accounting principle is summarized in Table 3.2. As summarized by Hunt:

Although Gordon's predictions of smoothing behavior motivated several empirical tests of the ISH [Income Smoothing Hypothesis], the results have been mixed and inconclusive. While methodological considerations may be partly to blame, the fact that the majority of the studies failed to control for ownership structure likely exacerbated the problem.[66]

Table 3.2
Ownership Structure and Accounting Choice

STUDY	SAMPLE	VARIABLES	MEASUREMENT OF OWNERSHIP STRUCTURE	METHODOLOGY	FINDINGS
Smith (1976)	110 firms (1954-1962)	5 measures of EPS, Accounting Changes	Owner or Manager controlled	Regression	Both owner controlled and manager controlled firms smooth income, but manager controlled firms are more likely to and do it more often
Kamin Ronen (1978)	310 U.S. Fortune 550 firms from 1965 list	Net operating income per share before fixed charges and extraordinary items, Net income before extraordinary items, Operating expenses, Ordinary expenses, Barriers to entry	2 way classification as owner or manager controlled	Regression	For high barrier to entry firms, manager controlled firms appear tɔ smooth income to a higher degree than owner controlled, for low barrier to entry firms, the opposite is true.
Salamon Smith (1979)	32 owner controlled and 32 manager controlled firms for 1954-1962	EPS, Security returns, Accounting policy decisions	Manager or Owner controlled	Regression	Managers in manager controlled firms attempt to control information in annual reports in a manner that misrepresents performance

Table 3.2 (Continued)

STUDY	SAMPLE	VARIABLES	MEASUREMENT OF OWNERSHIP STRUCTURE	METHODOLOGY	FINDINGS
Dhaliwal Salamon Smith (1982)	57 manager controlled firms and 53 owner controlled firms for 1959 and 1962	Deprecia-tion methods, Debt/Equity, Total assets	Manager or owner controlled	Probit	There exists a difference in depre-ciation methods adopted by manager and and owner controlled firms, manager controlled firms are more likely to choose methods which in-crease earnings
Belkaoui Picur (1984)	177 firms classified as peri-pheral or core	Various smoothing objectives and variables	N/A	Trend analysis	Higher degree of smoothing in peri-pheral firms
Niehaus (1989)	344 firms (1978-1982)	Assets, Book value of net assets, Debt/Equity, Inventory method	9 measures of owner-ship	Logit	When mana-gerial ownership is low, the likeli-hood of LIFO is negatively related to managerial ownership, and when manageri-al owner-ship is high, it is positively related
Haw Pastena Lilien (1990)	121 firms (1967-1980)	Market returns, Mergers	Owner or Manager controlled	Event-type Methodology	Information leakage varies with ownership control structure

OWNERSHIP STRUCTURE AND COMPENSATION

Theoretical Considerations

While management is assumed to act as a surrogate for owners, a substantial separation of ownership and control indicates a difference between the interests of owners and management.[67] In fact, various studies provide evidence supporting systematic differences between owner and management-controlled firms. Owner-controlled firms are reported to have higher profitability (see Table 3.1) and to replace executives more frequently when performance declines.[68] Management-controlled firms are reported to show a tendency toward over-reporting of earnings (see Table 3.2), and tend to be more risk-adverse (see Table 3.1). This evidence implies that for owner-controlled firms, the key determinant of the pay level of chief executives may be the owners themselves. With increasing levels of stock concentration, owners are in direct competition for the correct distribution of the total return of the firm and would vote a higher share for themselves. On the other hand, managers in manager controlled firms are more likely to view factors other than performance as the key basis of their pay. As summarized by Gomez-Mejia, Tosi, and Hinkin:

If these differences exist between management- and owner-controlled firms, it follows that type of control could be a key determinant of the pay levels of chief executives. Managers setting their pay levels relatively free of the influence of owners are . . . more likely to place their interests above those of owners, who impose little penalty.''[69]

Prior research on the determinants of executive compensation in large firms has concentrated on a functional view of the firm emphasizing size and performance. This view virtually ignores the importance of power as a key concept in the study of the large corporation. It has been speculated that CEOs tend to overcompensate themselves because of the unchallenged power that they enjoy within the organization. While power or control is derived from many sources, one cannot deny that the control of a significant block of stock of a firm enhances control.

Empirical Findings on Ownership Structure and Executive Compensation and Appraisal

Few empirical studies have assessed the role of ownership structure in the determination of executive compensation. Table 3.3 delineates the studies discussed here. Allen finds a significant relationship between executive power and compensation in a study that utilizes four control configurations based on stock ownership of corporate directors including the CEO.[70] The rationale behind his control configurations is as follows. CEOs are most powerful if they are the only individuals to control a significant block of stock (more than 5 percent), and slightly less powerful if no directors own a significant block. In these cases, the CEO tends to be overcompensated. CEOs are least powerful when

Table 3.3
Ownership Structure and Executive Compensation

STUDY	SAMPLE	VARIABLES	MEASUREMENT OF OWNERSHIP STRUCTURE	METHODOLOGY	FINDINGS
Allen (1981)	218 firms 1975, 1976	Firm size, Compensation	4 control configurations	Analysis of Covariance	Compensation is directly related to executive power
Gomez-Mejia Tosi Hinkin (1987)	71 large firms (1979-1982)	Compensation, Multiple performance and scale measures	Dummy variable for owner or manager control	Regression	Type of ownership significantly affects CEO pay
Tosi Gomez-Mejia (1989)	Survey of 175 chief compensation officers	Monitoring and incentive structure, compensation risk, Influence measures, Tenure, Outside hire, Size, Compensation	Owner or manager controlled based on survey questions	Regression Analysis of Covariance	In owner controlled firms there was more influence over CEO pay by major stockholders and boards of directors

other directors own a significant block of stock. In these cases, CEO control is tempered and they would tend to be paid less than their opportunity cost.

Gomez-Mejia, Tosi, and Hinkin[71] and Tosi and Gomez-Mejia[72] also found significant relationships between the type of ownership structure and executive compensation. (These two studies are discussed in Chapter 1.)

In light of conflicting findings on the role of sales and performance measures in the determination of executive compensation, ownership structure represents a potentially fruitful moderating variable.

NOTES

1. Adolf A. Berle and Gardiner C. Means, *The Modern Corporation and Private Property* (New York: Macmillan, 1932), p. 8.

2. E. F. Fama, "Agency Problems and the Theory of the Firm," *Journal of Political Economy* 88 (1980): 288.

3. Joshua Ronen and Simcha Sadan, *Smoothing Income Numbers, Objectives, Means, and Implications* (Reading, Mass.: Addison-Wesley, 1981), p. 1.

4. E. Daniel Smith, "The Effect of the Separation of Ownership from Control on Accounting Policy Decisions," *Accounting Review* 51/4 (1976): 707.

5. M. Schiff, "Accounting Tactics and the Theory of the Firm," *Journal of Accounting Research* 4 (1966): 62.

6. L. Gomez-Mejia, H. Tosi, and T. Hinkin, "Managerial Control, Performance and Executive Compensation," *Academy of Management Journal* 30 (1987): 54.

7. Michael P. Allen, "Power and Privilege in the Large Corporation," *American Journal of Sociology* 86/5 (1981): 1114.

8. Berle and Means, *Modern Corporation and Private Property*, p. 8.

9. See M. C. Jensen and W. H. Meckling, "Theory of the Firm and Managerial Behavior, Agency Costs, and Ownership Structure," *Journal of Financial Economics* 3 (1976): 305–60.

10. See H. Demsetz, "The Structure of Ownership and the Theory of the Firm," *Journal of Law and Economics* 26 (1983): 375–90.

11. Berle and Means, *Modern Corporation and Private Property*.

12. Jensen and Meckling, "Theory of the Firm and Managerial Behavior, Agency Costs, and Ownership Structure."

13. Demsetz, "Structure of Ownership and the Theory of the Firm."

14. E. F. Fama and M. C. Jensen, "Agency Problems and Residual Claims," *Journal of Law and Economics* 20 (1983): 327–49.

15. See Fama, "Agency Problems and the Theory of the Firm."

16. O. D. Hart, "The Market Mechanism as an Incentive Scheme," *Bell Journal of Economics* 14 (1983): 366–82.

17. M. Jensen and R. Ruback, "The Market for Corporate Control: The Scientific Evidence," *Journal of Financial Economics* 11 (1983): 5–50.

18. See R. A. Morck, A. Shleifer, and R. W. Vishny, "Management Ownership and Market Valuation: An Empirical Analysis," *Journal of Financial Economics* 20 (1988): 293–315; and A. Belkaoui and E. Pavlik, "The Effects of Ownership Structure and Diversification Strategy on Performance," *Managerial and Decision Economics* (forthcoming).

19. See, for example, D. R. Kamerschen, "The Influence of Ownership and Control on Profit Rates," *American Economic Review* 58 (1968): 432–47; R. J. Monsen, J. S. Chiu, and D. E. Cooley, "The Effect of Separation of Ownership and Control on the Performance of the Large Firm," *Quarterly Journal of Economics* 82 (1968): 435–51; K. J. Boudreaux, "Managerialism and Risk-Return Performance," *Southern Economic Journal* (Jan. 1973): 366–72; and Y. Amihud, J. Y. Kamin, and J. Ronen, " 'Managerialism,' 'Ownerism' and Risk," *Journal of Banking and Finance* 7 (1983): 189–96.

20. See J. Palmer, "The Profit-Performance Effects of the Separation of Ownership from Control in Large U.S. Industrial Corporations," *Bell Journal of Economics* (Spring 1973): 293–303; G. R. Salancik and J. Pfeffer, "The Effects of Ownership and Performance on Executive Tenure in U.S. Corporations," *Academy of Management Journal* 23 (1980): 653–64; and Morck, Shleifer, and Vishny, "Management Ownership and Market Valuation," for examples.

21. H. Demsetz and K. Lehn, "The Structure of Corporate Ownership: Theory and Consequences," *Journal of Political Economy* 93 (1985): 1155–77.

22. C. W. Hill and S. A. Snell, "Effects of Ownership Structure and Control on Corporate Productivity," *Academy of Management Journal* 32 (1989): 25–46.

23. Belkaoui and Pavlik, "Effects of Ownership Structure and Diversification Strategy on Performance."

24. For a discussion, see Boudreaux, "Managerialism and Risk-Return Performance."

25. See Morck, Shleifer, and Vishny, "Management Ownership and Market Valuation," pp. 293–315; and Belkaoui and Pavlik, "Effects of Ownership Structure and Diversification Strategy on Performance."

26. Herbert G. Hunt, "The Separation of Corporate Ownership and Control: Theory, Evidence, and Implications," *Journal of Accounting Literature* 5 (1986): 101.

27. Seer J. Cubbin and D. Leech, "The Effect of Shareholder Dispersion on the Degree of Control in British Companies: Theory and Measurement," *Economic Journal* 93 (1983): 351–69, for a discussion.

28. Hill and Snell, "Effects of Ownership Structure and Control on Corporate Productivity."

29. Morck, Shleifer, and Vishny, "Management Ownership and Market Valuation."

30. Demsetz and Lehn, "Structure of Corporate Ownership."

31. Belkaoui and Pavlik, "Effects of Ownership Structure and Diversification Strategy on Performance."

32. S. R. Hepworth, "Periodic Income Smoothing," *Accounting Review* (Jan. 1953): 34.

33. R. J. Monsen, Jr., and A. Downs, "A Theory of Large Managerial Firms," *Journal of Political Economy* 73 (1965): 221–236; Myron J. Gordon, "Postulates, Principles and Research in Accounting," *Accounting Review* (Apr. 1964): 251–63.

34. C. R. Beidleman, "Income Smoothing: The Role of Management," *Accounting Review* (Oct. 1973): 653.

35. Hepworth, "Periodic Income Smoothing," p. 34.

36. Gordon, "Postulates, Principles and Research in Accounting," 251–63.

37. Ibid.

38. Beidleman, "Income Smoothing," 653–57.

39. Ibid., p. 654.

40. Ibid.

41. R. Cyert and J. March, *A Behavioral Theory of the Firm* (Englewood Cliffs, N.J.: Prentice-Hall, 1963).

42. M. Schiff and A. Lewin, "Where Traditional Budgeting Fails," *Financial Executive* (May 1968): 57–62.

43. J. D. Thompson, *Organizations in Action* (New York: McGraw Hill, 1967).

44. J. Y. Kamin and J. Ronen, "The Smoothing of Income Numbers: Some Empirical Evidence on Systematic Differences among Management-Controlled and Owner-Controlled Firms," *Accounting Organizations and Society* 3/2 (1978): 141–53.

45. A. Barnea, J. Ronen, and S. Sadan, "Classificatory Smoothing of Income with Extraordinary Items," *Accounting Review* (Jan. 1976): 110–22.

46. Ibid.

47. A. Belkaoui, *Behavioral Accounting* (Westport, Conn.: Greenwood, 1989).

48. See Maureen McNichols and G. Peter Wilson, "Evidence of Earnings Management from the Provision for Bad Debts," *Accounting Review* (Supplement 1988): 1–31; and Paul M. Healy, "The Effect of Bonus Schemes on Accounting Decisions," *Journal of Accounting and Economics* 7 (1985): 85–107.

49. L. DeAngelo, "Managerial Competition, Information Costs, and Corporate Gov-

ernance: The Use of Accounting Performance Measures in Proxy Contests," *Journal of Accounting and Economics* (Jan. 1988): 3–36.

50. J. Jones, "The Effect of Foreign Trade Regulation on Accounting Choices and Production and Investment Decisions" (working paper, 1988).

51. Paul E. Dascher, and R. Malcolm, "A Note on Income Smoothing in the Chemical Industry," *Journal of Accounting Research* (Fall 1970): 253–54.

52. M. J. Gordon, "Discussion of the Effects of Alternative Accounting Rules for Nonsubsidiary Investments," *Journal of Accounting Research* 4 (Supplement 1966): 223.

53. R. M. Copeland, "Income Smoothing, Empirical Research in Accounting: Selected Studies," *Journal of Accounting Research* 6 (Supplement 1968): 101.

54. Barnea, Ronen, and Sadan, "Classificatory Smoothing of Income with Extraordinary Items," 111.

55. G. White, "Discretionary Accounting Decisions and Income Normalization," *Journal of Accounting Research* (Fall 1970): 260–74.

56. R. M. Copeland and Ralph D. Licastro, "A Note on Income Smoothing," *Accounting Review* (July 1968): 540–45.

57. Ibid., p. 542.

58. Barnea, Ronen, and Sadan, "Classificatory Smoothing of Income with Extraordinary Items," p. 111.

59. Copeland, "Income Smoothing, Empirical Research in Accounting," pp. 101–16.

60. Beidleman, "Income Smoothing," p. 658.

61. E. M. Beck, P. M. Horan, and C. M. Tolbert, III, "Stratification in a Dual Economy: A Sectoral Model of Earnings Determination," *American Sociological Review* (Oct. 1978): 704–20.

62. B. Harrison, "The Theory of the Dual Economy," in *The Worker in "Post Industrial" Capitalism*, eds. B. Silverman and M. Yanovitch (New York: Free Press, 1974), p. 280.

63. R. Hodson and R. L. Kaufman, "Economic Dualism: A Critical Review," *American Sociological Review* (Dec. 1982): 729.

64. Kamin and Ronen, "Smoothing of Income Numbers."

65. A. Belkaoui and R. Picur, "The Smoothing of Income Numbers: Some Empirical Evidence on Systematic Differences Between Core and Periphery Industrial Sectors," *Journal of Business Finance and Accounting* 11/4 (1984): 527–45.

66. Hunt, "Separation of Corporate Ownership and Control," p. 114.

67. See Berle and Means, *Modern Corporation and Private Property*.

68. Salancik and Pfeffer, "Effects of Ownership and Performance on Executive Tenure in U.S. Corporations," pp. 653–64.

69. Gomez-Mejia, Tosi, and Hihkin, "Managerial Control, Performance and Executive Compensation," p. 54.

70. Allen, "Power and Privilege in the Large Corporation."

71. Gomez-Mejia, Tosi, and Hinkin, "Managerial Control, Performance and Executive Compensation."

72. H. L. Tosi and L. R. Gomez-Mejia, "The Decoupling of CEO Pay and Performance: An Agency Theory Perspective," *Administrative Science Quarterly* 34 (1989): 169–89.

REFERENCES

Allen, Michael Patrick. 1981. Power and privilege in the large corporation. *American Journal of Sociology* 86 (5): 1112–1123.

Amihud, Y., J. Y. Kamin and J. Ronen. 1983. "Managerialism," "ownerism" and risk. *Journal of Banking and Finance* 7: 189–196.

Belkaoui, A. and E. Pavlik. 1990. The effects of ownership structure and diversification strategy on performance. Working Paper. University of Illinois at Chicago.

Belkaoui, A. and R. Picur. 1984. The smoothing of income numbers: Some empirical evidence on systematic differences between core and periphery industrial sectors. *Journal of Business Finance and Accounting* 11 (4): 527–545.

Boudreaux, K. J. 1973. Managerialism and risk-return performance. *Southern Economic Journal* (January): 366–372.

Dann L. Y. and H. Deangelo. 1988. "Corporate Financial Policy and Corporate Control." *Journal of Financial Economics* 20: 87–127.

Demsetz, H. and K. Lehn. 1985. The structure of corporate ownership: Theory and consequences. *Journal of Political Economy* 93: 1155–1177.

Dhaliwal, D. S., G. L. Salamon, and E. D. Smith. 1982. "The Effect of Owner versus Management Control on the Choice of Accounting Methods." *Journal of Accounting and Economics* 4: 41–53.

Gomez-Mejia, L., H. Tosi and T. Hinkin. 1987. Managerial control, performance and executive compensation. *Academy of Management Journal* 30: 51–70.

Haw, I., V. S. Pastena and S. B. Lilien. 1990. Market manifestation of nonpublic information prior to mergers: The effect of ownership structure. *The Accounting Review* 65 (2): 432–451.

Hill, C. W. and S. A. Snell. 1989. Effects of ownership structure and control on corporate productivity. *Academy of Management Journal* 32: 25–46.

Hodson, R. and R. L. Kaufman. 1982. Economic dualism: A critical review. *American Sociological Review* (December): 727–739.

Holderness, C. G. and D. P. Sheehan. 1988. "The Role of Majority Shareholders in Publicly Held Corporations." *Journal of Financial Economics* 20: 317–346.

Kamin, J. Y. and J. Ronen. 1978. The smoothing of income numbers: Some empirical evidence on systematic differences among management-controlled and owner-controlled firms. *Accounting Organizations and Society* 3 (2): 141–153.

Kamerschen, D. R. 1968. The influence of ownership and control on profit rates. *American Economic Review* 58: 432–447.

Kole, S. R. 1990. "A Reexamination of the Interaction Between Board Ownership of Equity and Firm Performance." Working Paper. University of Chicago.

Monsen, R. J., J. S. Chiu and D. E. Cooley. 1968. The effect of separation of ownership and control on the performance of the large firm. *Quarterly Journal of Economics* 82: 435–451.

Morck, R. A., A. Shleifer and R. W. Vishny. 1988. Management ownership and market valuation: an empirical analysis. *Journal of Financial Economics* 20: 293–315.

Niehaus, G. R. 1989. Ownership structure and inventory method choice. *The Accounting Review* 64: 269–284.

Palmer, J. 1973. The profit-performance effects of the separation of ownership from control in large U.S. industrial corporations. *Bell Journal of Economics* (Spring): 293–303.

Salamon, G. R. and E. D. Smith. 1979. Corporate control and managerial misrepresentation of firm performance. *Bell Journal of Economics* (Spring): 319–328.

Salancik, G. R. and J. Pfeffer. 1980. The effects of ownership and performance on executive tenure in U.S. corporations. *Academy of Management Journal* 23: 653–664.

Smith, A. 1989. "Corporate Ownership Structure and Performance: The Case of Management Buyouts." Working paper. University of Chicago.

Smith, E. Daniel. 1976. The effect of the separation of ownership from control on accounting policy decisions. *The Accounting Review* 51 (4): 707–722.

Tosi, H. and L. R. Gomez-Mejia. 1989. The decoupling of CEO pay and performance: An agency theory perspective. *Administrative Science Quarterly* 34: 169–189.

4

CEO COMPENSATION:
TOWARD A PATH MODEL

The determinants of executive compensation have been a topic of research interest in the accounting, finance, management, and economic literature since the early 1960s. CEOs rank at or near the top in terms of salaries by profession in the United States. It is no wonder that their compensation arrangements have come under critical review. Questions concerning whether the resources of the firm are being efficiently used by those in control in light of the high compensation afforded these individuals are prevalent in the business press. Although prior research[1] has examined variables such as firm size and firm performance measures in hopes of establishing a relationship of pay to performance or size, it has failed to examine these variables in terms of the organizational and ownership structure of the firm. Differences in the internal organizational structure of a firm, based upon differences in diversification strategies, have been associated with differences in firm performance.[2] Furthermore, as pointed out by Gomez-Mejia, Tosi, and Hinkin, "previous research on the relationship between compensation to CEOs and factors like size and performance has produced weak relationships with company performance. Research focusing on distribution of ownership, however, provides a potentially useful theoretical departure."[3]

In order to examine the combined effects of the variables of interest—firm performance, organizational structure (in terms of diversification strategy), and ownership structure—on the determination of executive compensation, path analysis is employed. The analysis proceeds in two steps. The first step includes the use of regression analysis to test for the effects of all independent variables on executive compensation. Since the research model proposed postulates the existence of both indirect and direct effects of certain variables, it is a partial mediation model. Therefore, the second step relies on path analysis, the appropriate technique in the case of a partial mediation model,[4] to assess the significance of both direct and indirect effects of the variables on executive compensation. This model may be a first step toward the development of a more comprehensive model and/or theory of the determinants of executive compensation. The innovation of this model is in the integration of three theoretical research areas: the m-form hypothesis (see Chapter 2), the ownership structure thesis (see Chapter 3), and the compensation thesis (see Chapter 1).

The intent of this study is twofold: (1) to construct a path analytic model that integrates both the direct and indirect effects of the structural variables of diversification strategy, ownership structure, and firm performance on executive compensation; and (2) to empirically test this model on recent (1987) data for a large sample of U.S. Fortune 500 firms.

This study contributes to the existing literature in several ways. First, it provides a more comprehensive model of the determination of executive compensation by examining both indirect and direct effects of determinants previously examined separately, but now embodied in a more complex path analytic model. In particular, the roles of firm performance and diversification strategy as both direct and indirect determinants are examined. Concurrent with this, the influence of ownership structure as a direct determinant, and possibly one mediated by firm performance and diversification, is empirically tested. The compensation of the top executives in large U.S. corporations is determined in a complex fashion, and merits a comprehensive analysis of the relationships of ownership structure, diversification, and firm performance measures.

Furthermore, this study addresses questions arising from prior research on compensation, and the results may have implications for future work. Specifically, different measures of the variables of interest (ownership structure, performance, and diversification) are employed in an attempt to assess the appropriateness of measurement. Future work, employing the model described herein, can incorporate the influence of other variables emanating not only from the firm itself but also from the outside environment.

LIMITATIONS AND INTEGRATION

The Executive Compensation Thesis

Table 1.2 summarizes studies related to the determination of the functional form of executive compensation. Although profitability (measured in terms of absolute profit and profit rate) shows up as an important predictor of executive compensation in some studies, company size as measured by sales is also an important determinant. This may be due in part to discretionary decisions of managers that affect the determination of profit more than sales in a large firm. In other words, there still does not exist overwhelming evidence that supports the sales maximization or profit maximization hypothesis, as discussed in Chapter 1. It should also be noted that studies differ in their measurement of compensation and performance.

The inconclusive results of empirical studies of executive compensation may be due to the way in which the performance variables are defined or the restriction of independent variables to sales and profitability measures. In either case there is a need to update these findings with different measures of size and performance. This study assesses the relationship of performance measures and compensation, and also considers the effect of other variables on the determination of executive compensation based upon the rationales offered by agency theory.

The M-Form Hypothesis and Diversification

Tables 2.2 and 2.3 summarize previous empirical research on the relationship of diversification, firm performance, and risk. While previous research has tended to support the proposition that m-form reorganization positively affects performance, some recent research has produced mixed evidence.[5]

Inconclusive studies on the relationship between multidivisional structure and firm performance may be due in part to failure to consider the underlying economic objectives of various diversification strategies. Hoskisson suggests that the "distinction between functionally structured firms and M-form firms is too simple because all diversification strategies do not have the same economic intent."[6] His study focuses on developing and testing a contingency perspective in which implementation of an m-form structure is related to performance under three different diversification strategies: vertical integration, related diversification, and unrelated diversification. Each strategy involves a different economic objective. In the case of vertical integration, firms are seeking to increase economies of scale and efficiency. When a related diversification strategy is embraced, the intent is to exploit economies of scope through the sharing of resources and capabilities. The objective of an unrelated diversification strategy is more efficient capital reallocation, that is, the development and operation of an internal capital market in which efficient resource allocations are made to specific divisions, as opposed to economies of scale or scope. The central proposition in Hoskisson's contingency theory is that implementation of an m-form structure affects performance differently depending on the strategy existing before implementation. Hoskisson finds that m-form adaption increases rate of return for unrelated diversifiers, but decreases rate of return for related diversifiers. In the case of related diversifiers, the change is not significant.

In light of Hoskisson's findings and the aforementioned number of ways to measure diversification, there is a need to reexamine findings on the m-form hypothesis. This study does so by assessing the impact of both related diversification and unrelated diversification on performance of the large firm, and the pay afforded their CEOs.

Ownership Structure

Even though vigorous debate on the potential effect of ownership structure and control on firm performance has been engaged in theoretically, few empirical studies have focused on this relationship. This is due in part to difficulties encountered in meaningfully measuring the distribution of stock ownership in a firm. Studies that have been published yield conflicting results (see Chapter 3).

Prior research on ownership structure has relied to a great degree upon either a single dichotomous variable to contrast owner control and management control or the previously mentioned 1980 Corporate Data Exchange assemblance of data. There appears to be a need to reexamine the issue in light of previous conflicting findings with a more meaningful measurement of ownership structure. This study measures both stock concentration and management stockholdings from data gathered from the proxy statements of a large sample of Fortune 500 companies. Stock concentration is defined as the share of ownership by outside stockholders owning more than 5 percent of the voting common stock, while management stockholdings is defined as the percentage of common voting stock held by officers and directors. These continuous measurements of ownership structure are then utilized to reassess the role of ownership structure in firm performance, executive compensation, and diversification strategies.

RESEARCH MODELS AND HYPOTHESES

Figure 4.1 illustrates the initial research model, which incorporates the proposed role of ownership structure, diversification strategy, and firm performance in the determination of executive compensation. Each line represents a research hypothesis. For example, stock concentration, one proposed measure of ownership structure, is shown as influencing executive compensation both directly and indirectly through the mediators of diversification strategy, management stockholdings and firm performance.

Stock Concentration and Management Stockholdings

The model assumes that the interests of owners and managers are divergent. The distinction is based on the premise made in the literature on managerial discretion that views owners (stockholders) as wealth maximizers requiring a maximization of efficiency (and cost minimization). Managers, on the other hand, have a tendency to maximize a utility function having remuneration, power, and security as major arguments, requiring a maximization of firm size and diversity.[7] The model also assumes, as Berle and Means argue,[8] that stock concentration matters for firm performance. Dispersion of stockholders' ownership allows managers holding little equity in the firm to forego maximizing shareholder wealth to benefit their own interests rather than those of the stockholders. This is due to the existence of information asymmetries and, in the case of diffused stock ownership, the inability of the dispersed owners to remove managers.

In order to align the interests of owners and managers, stock-based compensation plans that increase management stockholdings have been utilized.[9] Given

Figure 4.1
Initial Research Model

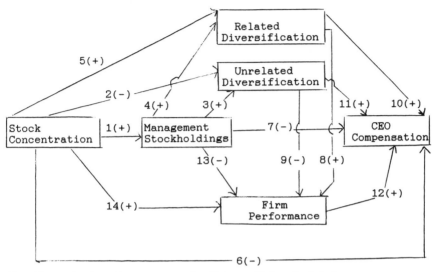

Note: The number for each path corresponds with its specific hypothesis in the text.

a choice, managers may not prefer such arrangements due to the risk and volatility introduced into their own remuneration. When stock concentration is high, owners have the ability to introduce the adoption of compensation plans that facilitate this alignment of interests by increasing the stake or holdings of management in the firm. Based upon the above rationale, we may expect the following:

Hypothesis 1: There will be a positive relationship between stock concentration and a firm's level of management stockholdings.

Ownership Structure and Diversification

The model distinguishes between the extent of two types of diversification based on product lines (related and unrelated) and two measures of ownership structure (stock concentration and management stockholdings). Prior research suggests that diversification into unrelated businesses is associated with both lower economic returns and lower risk than related diversification.[10] Given the divergent interests of managers and owners, the pursuit of an unrelated diversification strategy would serve managers with no equity in the firm in that it would maximize the size of the firm, leading to higher remuneration, power, and prestige, while at the same time diversifying employment risk. Stockholders, on the other hand, have little to gain from the risk-reducing aspects of unrelated diversification, since they can accomplish this by diversifying their own portfolio, and will avoid this strategy, which trades efficiency for an increase in firm size or product lines. Thus,

Hypothesis 2:   There will be a negative relationship between stock concentration and unrelated diversification.

Hypothesis 3:   There will be a positive relationship between the extent of management stockholdings and unrelated diversification.

Alternatively, diversification into related businesses has been associated both theoretically and empirically with superior economic performance due to more efficient utilization of firm resources (economies of scope and scale). This strategy appears congruent with the stockholders' desire to maximize efficiency. Thus we would expect that:

Hypothesis 4:   There will be a positive relationship between the extent of management stockholdings and related diversification.

Hypothesis 5:   There will be a positive relationship between stock concentration and related diversification.

Ownership Structure and Executive Compensation

Prior research on the determinants of executive compensation in large firms has concentrated on a functional view of the firm, emphasizing size and performance. This view ignores the importance of power as a key concept in the study of the large corporation. Allen argues that "the fact that chief executive officers often possess the power to influence their own levels of compensation has also been ignored." [11] Furthermore, the observed relationships among corporate size, profitability, and executive compensation are consistent with a "power" theory of organizational structure. It has been speculated that CEOs tend to overcompensate themselves because of the unchallenged power that they enjoy within the organization. While power or control is derived from many sources, one cannot deny that the control of a significant block of the stock of a firm enhances control. Allen finds a significant relationship between executive power and compensation in a study that utilizes four control configurations based on stock ownership of corporate directors, including the CEO. [12]

Building on the above, this study utilizes the level of stock concentration and management stockholdings to capture the notion of power or control in a firm, and tests the potential link between power and executive compensation. For owner-controlled firms, the key determinant of the pay level of chief executives rests with the owners themselves, who would tend to vote a higher share of the total return of the firm for themselves. Thus:

Hypothesis 6:   There will be a negative relationship between stock concentration and executive compensation.

Managers in manager-controlled firms are more likely to view factors other than performance as the key determinants of their pay.[13] Furthermore, managers holding enough voting power to guarantee their jobs may favor pay packages that include bonuses and long-term income as opposed to base salary. Thus:

Hypothesis 7:   There will be a negative relationship between the level of management stockholdings and executive compensation.

Firm Performance and Diversification

Empirical results on the effects of the implementation of a decentralized organizational structure on performance differentiate between the impact of related and unrelated diversification strategies on firm performance. Unrelated diversification is achieved when managers trade efficiency for an increase in firm size and decrease in operating risks.[14] In fact, empirical evidence shows that unrelated diversification is associated with lower economic return[15] and lower risk[16] than related diversification. On the other hand, both theory and empirical results indicate an association of related diversification with superior economic performance.[17] Thus:

Hypothesis 8:   There will be a positive relationship between firm performance and related diversification.

Hypothesis 9:   There will be a negative relationship between firm performance and unrelated diversification.

Executive Compensation and Diversification

Finkelstein and Hambrick suggest the interesting notion that compensation practices may drive diversification activity, and be a partial explanation for the often disappointing returns accrued.[18] With the exception of a study by Harris,[19] there is a noticeable absence in the literature of empirical findings on the possible effects of organizational structure on executive compensation. Harris's study views executive compensation as a potential form of discretionary behavior. The m-form of organizational structure is hypothesized to control opportunistic discretionary behavior better than the u-form. Utilizing time-series data for nineteen firms and a dummy variable for organizational structure, Harris finds evidence of a positive significant relationship between the decentralized form of organization and executive compensation. In addition, the control arrangements necessary to implement the decentralization are more complex and demanding than with a centralized organization.[20] Thus it is expected that:

Hypothesis 10: There will be a positive relationship between unrelated diversification and executive compensation.

Hypothesis 11: There will be a positive relationship between related diversification and executive compensation.

Firm Performance and Executive Compensation

There is ample evidence indicating a positive relationship between firm profitability and executive compensation (see Chapter 1). This evidence shows that the executive compensation committees of the board of directors, in their search for incentive arrangements that will encourage management to act in the shareholders' interests, set compensation on the basis of financial performance. This is also consistent with the evidence provided by Smith and Watts,[21] indicating that the compensation plans approved by the boards of directors generally link pay to performance measures that are themselves related to shareholder wealth. One such performance measure is the accounting profit of the firm. Antle and Smith present two reasons why accounting measures, as opposed to market measures, might be used.[22] The first is related to the fact that stock prices impound all information relevant for evaluating the performance of the firm's management.[23] The second reason is that it is easier for the executive to hedge the risk from a contract based on stock returns than one based on accounting variables. Both accounting- and market-based measures are used in this study. Thus:

Hypothesis 12: There will be a positive relationship between firm performance and executive compensation.

Ownership Structure and Firm Performance

Distinguishing again between the level of stock concentration and management stockholdings as measures of the ownership structure in a large firm, and relying on arguments advanced in Chapter 3 on the convergence-of-interests hypothesis and the entrenchment hypothesis, we would expect that:

Hypothesis 13: There will be a negative relationship between a firm's financial performance and management stockholdings held at high ranges.

Hypothesis 14: There will be a positive relationship between a firm's performance and stock concentration held at high ranges.

The Effects of Size

Figure 4.2 illustrates the initial research model, incorporating the proposed role of firm size on the determination of executive compensation. The effects of firm size on diversification strategy, firm performance, and CEO compen-

Figure 4.2
Research Model with Size Included

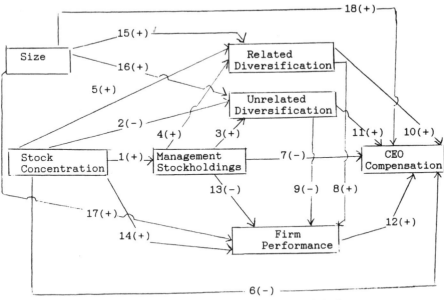

Note: The number for each path corresponds with its specific hypothesis in the text.

sation are well established in the literature. First, the effect of size on either related diversification or unrelated diversification strategy is positive in the sense that both strategies possibly imply a growing and expanding firm.[24] Therefore,

Hypothesis 15: There will be a positive relationship between a firm's size and related diversification.

Hypothesis 16: There will be a positive relationship between a firm's size and unrelated diversification.

Second, the effect of size on performance is positive in the sense that bigger firms have more resources to devote to profitable opportunities. The alternate hypothesis may be that bigger firms have more obsolete assets that hinder profitability. Therefore,

Hypothesis 17: There will be a positive relationship between a firm's size and financial performance.

Third, the effect of size on CEO compensation is positive because of two possible rationales; (1) bigger firms tend to pay more because the CEO oversees substantial resources;[25] and (2) bigger firms have the ability to pay more.[26] Thus

Hypothesis 18: There will be a positive relationship between a firm's size and CEO compensation.

DATA, SAMPLE, AND METHODOLOGY

Our hypotheses suggest that ownership structure and firm size affect CEO compensation directly. They also suggest that ownership structure and firm size affect executive compensation indirectly through the impact of stockholder and manager preferences on diversification strategy and firm performance. Given that both direct and indirect effects are postulated within the framework of the causal model, the model is a partial mediation model and path analysis is the appropriate analytical strategy.[27]

Initial Sample Determination

The data were drawn from the Fortune 500 as of April 25, 1988, and the *Investment Outlook Scoreboard*, published by *Business Week* as of December 28, 1986, and December 28, 1987. Furthermore, the firm's chief executive officer had to be included in *Business Week*'s "Corporate Elite," as of October 21, 1988. The initial sample resulted in the inclusion of 247 Fortune 500 companies, for which all data were available, representing twenty-eight industries. Data on 1987 annual compensation for the CEO, sales, profits, assets, and market values were compiled for each firm from the above-named sources.

Measurement of Variables

Executive Compensation

As in previous studies, this study utilizes cash compensation (salary plus bonus) as the measure of executive compensation. While cash compensation is not a complete measure, it typically represents 70 to 80 percent of a CEO's annual compensation. Furthermore, as demonstrated by Lewellen and Huntsman,[28] a more comprehensive measure of executive compensation does not perform any better than salary plus cash bonus.

Ownership Structure

This study attempts to capture the ownership structure of a firm in terms of two continuous variables, stock concentration and management stockholdings. The stock concentration variable is computed as the share of ownership by outside stockholders owning more than 5 percent of the common voting stock, while management stockholdings are to be measured by the percentage of common stock held by officers and directors. Prior research on the role of owner-ship structure in the performance of a firm and the determination of executive compensation has yielded mixed results that may be attributable to the mea-surement of these variables.

This study avoids invoking arbitrary criteria in defining the size of a control-ling stockholding and relying on a single dichotomous variable to contrast owner and manager control. Furthermore, it does not rely upon the 1980 data assem-bled by the Corporate Data Exchange. Instead, the data for the ownership struc-ture variables were collected from the individual 1988 proxy statements of the firms involved in the sample.

Diversification

Various measures of diversification have been utilized in prior work, all of which can be described as either strategy-based categorical methods or contin-uous count measures based on SIC codes. Strategy-based measures, popular-ized by Rumelt,[29] rely on underlying logic rather than the number of businesses in which a company operates in measuring diversification. To date, there is no generally accepted method of operationalizing the measurement of diversifica-tion, and empirical evidence[30] suggests that neither type is clearly superior to the other. While strategy-based categorical measurements have been touted as considering both qualitative and quantitative factors, business count measures have become more sophisticated and are viewed as more objective. Further-more, the availability of data and time factor make SIC-based diversification measures more advantageous in large cross-sectional studies. For these reasons, this study will utilize business count methods in measuring related diversifica-tion and unrelated diversification. Data to compute these measures were ob-tained from Dunn and Bradstreet's *Reference Book of Corporate Management*.

Firm Performance and Size

To parallel previous empirical work the performance of the firm is measured in both accounting terms (as profit over assets [rate of return on assets]) and market terms (as market capitalization). Market capitalization is defined as the product of the number of outstanding shares and the price per common share at the end of the year. Again both measurements are computed and the results compared for the companies sampled.

Firm size is measured alternatively as total sales, total assets, and market capitalization.

NOTES

1. See, for example, R. Antle and A. Smith, "An Empirical Investigation of the Relative Performance Evaluation of Corporate Executives," *Journal of Accounting Re-search* 24/1 (1986); D. Ciscel and T. Carroll, "The Determinants of Executive Salaries: An Econometric Survey," *Review of Economics and Statistics* (Feb. 1980); A. Cosh,

"The Remuneration of Chief Executives in the United Kingdom," *Economics Journal* 85 (Mar. 1975); K. Ely, "Cross-Sectional Variations in the Relationship Between Accounting Variables and the Chief Executive's Compensation" (working paper, University of Chicago, 1988); T. D. Hogan and L. R. McPheters, "Executive Compensation: Performance vs. Personal Characteristics," *Southern Economic Journal* 46 (1980); Richard A. Lambert and David F. Larker, "An Analysis of the Use of Accounting and Market Measures of Performance in Executive Compensation Contracts," *Journal of Accounting Research* 25 (Supplement 1987); W. G. Lewellen and B. Huntsman, "Managerial Pay and Corporate Performance," *American Economic Review* (Sept. 1970); R. T. Masson, "Executive Incomes, Sales and Profits," *Journal of Political Economy* (Dec. 1971); Joseph W. McGuire, John S. Chiu, and Alvar O. Elbing, "Executive Incomes, Sales and Profits," *American Economic Review* 52 (Sept. 1962); and Kevin Murphy, "Corporate Performance and Managerial Remuneration: An Empirical Analysis," *Journal of Accounting and Economics* (Apr. 1985).

2. See Oliver E. Williamson, *The Economic Institutions of Capitalism* (New York: Free Press, 1985); Alfred D. Chandler, *Strategy and Structure* (Cambridge, Mass.: MIT, 1962); and Oliver E. Williamson, *Markets and Hierarchies: Analysis and Antitrust Implications* (New York: Free Press, 1975).

3. Luis R. Gomez-Mejia, Henry Tosi, and Timothy Hinkin, "Managerial Control, Performance and Executive Compensation," *Academy of Management Journal* 30/1 (1987): 55.

4. See L. R. James and J. M. Brett, "Mediators, Moderators and Tests for Mediation," *Journal of Applied Psychology* 69 (1984): 307–21, for a discussion.

5. Robert E. Hoskisson, "Multidivisional Structure and Performance: The Contingency of Diversification Strategy," *Academy of Management Journal* 30/4 (1987): 625–44.

6. Ibid., p. 626.

7. See M. Aoki, *The Co-Operative Game Theory of the Firm* (Oxford, England: Clarendon, 1984); A. Belkaoui, *Conceptual Foundations of Management Accounting* (Reading, Mass.: Addison-Wesley, 1980); J. K. Galbraith, *The New Industrial State* (New York: New American Library, 1967); R. Marris, *The Economic Theory of Managerial Capitalism* (London: Macmillan, 1967); and O. E. Williamson, *The Economics of Discretionary Behavior* (Englewood Cliffs, N.J.: Prentice-Hall, 1964).

8. A. A. Berle and G. C. Means, *The Modern Corporation* (New York: Macmillan, 1932).

9. See H. Demsetz, "The Structure of Ownership and the Theory of the Firm," *Journal of Law and Economics* 26 (1983): 375–90; and W. Lewellen, C. Loderer, and A. Rosenfeld, "Merger Decisions and Executive Stock Ownership in Acquiring Firms," *Journal of Accounting and Economics* 7 (Apr. 1985): 209–31.

10. See H. Kurt Christensen and Cynthia A. Montgomery, "Corporate Economic-Performance: Diversification Strategy vs. Market Structure," *Strategic Management Journal* 2 (1981); Richard A. Bettis and Bijay Mahajan, "Risk/Return Performance of Diversified Firms," *Management Science* 31/7 (1985); Raphael Amit and Joshua Livnat, "Diversification and the Risk-Return Trade-Off," *Academy of Management Journal* 31/1 (1988); Richard P. Rumelt, "Diversification Strategy and Profitability," *Strategic Management Journal* 3 (1982); and Richard P. Rumelt, *Strategy, Structure, and Economic Performance* (Cambridge, Mass.: Harvard University Press, 1974).

11. Michael P. Allen, "Power and Privilege in the Large Corporation," *American Journal of Sociology* 86/5 (1981): 1114.

12. Ibid., pp. 1112–23.

13. Gomez-Mejia, Tosi, and Hinkin, "Managerial Control, Performance and Executive Compensation," pp. 51–70.

14. Marris, *Economic Theory of Managerial Capitalism.*

15. See Christensen and Montgomery, "Corporate Economic Performance," pp. 327–343; and Rumelt, "Diversification Strategy and Profitability," pp. 359–369, and *Strategy, Structure, and Economic Performance.*

16. See Amit and Livnat, "Diversification and the Risk Return Trade-Off," pp. 154–66; and Bettis and Mahajan, "Risk/Return Performance of Diversified Firms," pp. 785–89.

17. See R. A. Bettis, "Performance Differences in Related and Unrelated Diversified Firms," *Strategic Management Journal* 2 (1981): 379–93; Christensen and Montgomery, "Corporate Economic Performance," pp. 327–43; and Rumelt, "Diversification Strategy and Profitability," pp. 359–69, and *Strategy, Structure, and Economic Performance.*

18. S. Finkelstein and D. C. Hambrick, "Chief Executive Compensation: A Synthesis and Reconciliation," *Strategic Management Journal* 9 (1988): 543–58.

19. Barry C. Harris, *Organization, The Effect on Large Corporations* (Ann Arbor, Mich.: UMI Research Press, 1983).

20. Charles W. L. Hill and Robert E. Hoskisson, "Strategy and Structure in the Multiproduct Firm," *Academy of Management Review* 12/2 (1987).

21. C. Smith and R. Watts, "Incentive and Tax Effects of Executive Compensation Plans," *Australian Journal of Management* 7 (1982): 139–57.

22. R. Antle and A. Smith, "Measuring Executive Compensation: Methods and an Application," *Journal of Accounting Research* (Spring 1985): 296–325.

23. Ibid.

24. Hoskisson, "Multidivisional Structure and Performance," pp. 625–44.

25. Finkelstein and Hambrick, "Chief Executive Compensation," pp. 543–48.

26. Ciscel and Carroll, "Determinants of Executive Salaries," pp. 7–13.

27. James and Brett, "Mediators, Moderators and Tests for Mediation," pp. 307–21.

28. Lewellen and Huntsman, "Managerial Pay and Corporate Performance," pp. 710–20.

29. Rumelt, "Diversification Strategy and Profitability," pp. 359–69, and *Strategy, Structure, and Economic Performance.*

30. C. Montgomery, "The Measurement of Firm Diversification: Some New Empirical Evidence," *Academy of Management Journal* 25/2 (1982): 299–307.

5

THE CEO COMPENSATION MODEL: REGRESSION AND PATH MODEL RESULTS

The final sample included 216 companies from 28 different industries. The appendix includes the data utilized in this study on executive compensation, firm sales, firm performance, diversification, and ownership structure for the year 1987. In addition, the appendix includes other information on the CEOs sampled (age, tenure with the company, and tenure as CEO). Table 5.1 summarizes relevant statistics on the variables utilized based upon available data for firms included in the sample.

The analysis proceeds in two steps. The first step involves the use of regression analysis to test the effects of all the independent variables on executive compensation; the second relies upon path analysis to test for the direct and indirect effects of ownership structure and firm size on executive compensation. In each step the logarithm of the compensation variable and the performance variable is used. Both variables, before transformation, are skewed to the right. As suggested by Neter and Wasserman,[1] if the distribution of the variables is skewed to the right, using a logarithmic transformation helps to normalize them. Table 5.2 gives the correlation for all variables.

The approach taken in each step involves running separate models in which the compensation variable remains unadjusted for assets and deflated by total assets in an effort to control for company size. Furthermore, in an effort to discern the role of firm size, total sales and total assets are included as independent variables. Firm performance is measured in terms of both accounting (return on assets) and market (market value over assets) measures to assess the sensitivity of the results in each case to alternative measures.

Finally, following the different results obtained by Morck, Shleifer, and Vishny[2] and Demsetz and Lehn,[3] both piecewise linear regression and strictly linear regression models are tested with regard to the ownership structure variables.

Table 5.1
Mean Values and Standard Deviations for Variables

Variable	N	Mean	Standard Deviation
Compensation	216	852.269	369.15
Ownership Structure:			
Management Stockholdings	197	6.888	11.33
Stock Concentration	197	12.354	17.85
Diversification:			
Related	216	2.519	1.46
Unrelated	216	1.940	1.28
Profits	216	276.609	670.79
Market Value	216	4161.007	7141.85
Total Assets	216	4802.744	10043.30
Sales	216	5247.341	10587.41

Note: Fortune 500 companies, 1987.

REGRESSION MODELS

The Nonmonotonic Model Without Assets

The results of two regression equations, one with performance measured as the logarithm of profit over assets and one for performance measured as the logarithm of market value over book value of total assets, are reported in Table 5.3. Both are piecewise linear regression equations in that turning points of 5 and 25 percent are utilized with respect to the ownership structure variables of management stockholdings and stock concentration. Neither equation includes total assets or a proxy for firm size as an independent variable.

The results of both equations are significant and explain an adequate amount of variance. The signs in both equations with regard to diversification and firm performance are as expected. However, the only significant ownership structure variable is management stockholdings of 5 percent or less. Furthermore, the signs on the ownership structure variables are not as expected, and differ depending upon the performance measure utilized. Since little evidence as to a significant nonmonotonic relationship exists, the analysis proceeds to test a strictly linear relationship.

Table 5.2
Pearson Correlations for All Variables

Variables	1	2	3	4	5	6	7	8
1. Executive Compensation								
2. Management Stockholdings	-.206***							
3. Stock Concentration	-.251***	.178**						
4. Related Diversification	.158**	-.096	-.109					
5. Unrelated Diversification	.073	-.029	-.006	-.486***				
6. Profits over Assets	.162**	.203***	-.116	-.007	-.280***			
7. Market Value over Assets	.087	.161**	-.091	.052	-.293***	.711***		
8. Assets	.264***	-.174**	.173**	-.027	.172**	-.167**	-.262***	
9. Sales	.277***	-.168**	.176**	.012	.143**	-.153**	-.257***	.979***

*p < .10
**p < .05
***p < .01

The Strictly Linear Model Without Assets

The results of the linear regression model with alternative measures of firm performance are summarized in Table 5.4. These results, as opposed to those of the piecewise regression, show all independent variables to be significant. Both equations explain an adequate amount of variance and the signs of the coefficients are as expected.

The Nonmonotonic Model with Size as a Deflator

The next step in the analysis involves deflating the dependent variable (log executive compensation) by company size. Alternative measurements of size—

Table 5.3
Results of Piecewise Regression Analysis[a]

Independent Variables	Regression # 1 [b]	Regression # 2 [c]
Related Diversification	0.03912	0.05815
	(2.036) **	(2.880) *
Unrelated Diversification	0.07007	0.07671
	(3.041) *	(3.187) *
Management Stockholdings:		
0-5%	-0.04504	-0.03524
	(-2.718) *	(-1.983) **
5-25%	0.00497	-0.00511
	(0.851)	(-0.862)
Over 25%	-0.00361	0.00174
	(-0.738)	(0.335)
Stock Concentration:		
0-5%	-0.01084	-0.01709
	(-0.848)	(-1.253)
5-25%	-0.00519	-0.00355
	(-1.107)	(-0.710)
Over 25%	-0.00133	-0.00087
	(-0.481)	(-0.312)
Profit over Assets (log)	0.12744	-----
	(2.474) **	
Market Value over Total Assets (log)	-----	0.08695
		(1.982) **
R^2 (Adjusted)	13.92%	15.86%
F	4.306 *	5.105 *

[a]T-statistics are in parentheses. The significance levels are indicated as follows: * for $< .01$, ** for $< .05$, and *** for $< .10$.
[b]Regression 1 is where performance is measured as the logarithm of profit over assets.
[c]Regression 2 is where performance is measured as the logarithm of market value over total assets.

total assets, total sales, and market value—are utilized to assess the sensitivity of the results. Once again, the resulting regression equations are run utilizing two alternative measures of firm performance, the log of profit over assets and the log of market value over assets. This procedure yields six alternative regression equations for the piecewise model, the results of which are presented in Table 5.5.

Once again, diversification and firm performance variables are significant whether compensation (the dependent variable) is deflated by total assets, total sales, or market value. However, the coefficients on the diversification variables are negative when total assets or market value is used as a deflator. Furthermore, the coefficients for both performance measures are negative when total sales is used as a deflator.

With regard to the ownership structure variables, management stockholdings

Table 5.4
Results of Linear Regression Analysis [a]

Independent Variables	Regression # 1 [b]	Regression # 2 [c]
Related Diversification	0.1781	0.2367
	(2.095) **	(2.971)*
Unrelated Diversification	0.2653	0.2656
	(3.064) **	(3.262)*
Management Stockholdings	-0.1248	-0.1651
	(-1.731) ***	(-2.452) **
Stock Concentration	-0.2097	-0.1793
	(-2.926) *	(-2.617)*
Profit over Assets (log)	0.1878	——
	(2.527) **	——
Market Value over Total Assets (log)	——	0.1577
	——	(2.245) **
R ^{2} (adjusted)	11.52%	13.5%
F	5.791 *	7.143 *

[a] Standardized betas are reported. T-statistics are in parentheses. The significance levels are indicated as follows: *for <.01, **for <.05, and ***for <.10.
[b] Regression 1 is where performance is measured as the logarithm of profit over assets.
[c] Regression 2 is where performance is measured as the logarithm of market value over total assets.

in the 0–5 percent range are significant and positively related to the compensation variable for all variations of the model. The 5–25 percent range is significant and negative in all cases when performance is measured in terms of the logarithm of market value over total assets, but only when compensation is deflated by total sales, in the case where performance is measured in terms of the logarithm of profits over assets. All other ranges of management stockholdings are insignificant.

Stock concentration in the 0–5 percent range is only significant and positively related to compensation when compensation is deflated by total assets and the accounting measure of performance utilized. This range of holdings is insignificant in all other variations of the model. The 5–25 percent range for stock concentration is significant and positively related to compensation as de-

Table 5.5
Results of Piecewise Regression Analysis[a]

Dependent Variable - Log (Compensation/Total Assets)

Independent Variables	Regression # 1 [b]	Regression # 2 [c]
Related Diversification	-0.11375	-0.08668
	(-2.519) **	(-2.018) **
Unrelated Diversification	-0.17938	-0.14010
	(-3.312) *	(-2.736) *
Management Stockholdings:		
0-5%	0.19692	0.21771
	(5.055) *	(5.756) *
5-25%	-0.01783	-0.03086
	(-1.296)	(-2.445) **
Over 25%	0.00245	0.00459
	(0.212)	(0.415)
Stock Concentration:		
0-5%	0.05211	0.03247
	(1.733) ***	(1.118)
5-25%	0.01869	0.02720
	(1.694) ***	(2.557) **
Over 25%	0.00218	-0.00197
	(0.336)	(-0.332)
Profit over Assets (log)	0.63282	-----
	(5.225) *	
Market Value over Total Assets (log)	-----	0.65578
		(7.024) *
R^2 (Adjusted)	39.39%	42.55%
F	14.288 *	17.127 *

flated by total assets or total sales for both performance measures, but not in the case where compensation is deflated by market value. The over 25 percent range of stock concentration is insignificant in all variations of this model.

Overall, all six equations tested in this part of the analysis are significant and explain a great deal of variance.

The Strictly Linear Model with Size as a Deflator

The analysis next tests a strictly linear regression model in which compensation, the dependent variable, is deflated by the three alternative proxies for firm size. Both accounting and market measures of performance are employed. The results of the six alternative regression equations are summarized in Table 5.6.

All of the equations tested in this part of the analysis are significant and explain an adequate amount of variance. Also, all of the independent variables are significant for the alternative models tested with the exception of stock

Table 5.5 (Continued)

Dependent Variable - Log (Compensation/Total Sales)

Independent Variables	Regression # 1 [b]	Regression # 2 [c]
Related Diversification	-0.09427 (-2.068) **	-0.08668 (-2.018) **
Unrelated Diversification	-0.12485 (-2.283) **	-0.14010 (-2.736) *
Management Stockholdings:		
0-5%	0.20502 (5.213) *	0.21771 (5.756) *
5-25%	-0.03236 (-2.331) **	-0.03086 (-2.445) **
Over 25%	0.00630 (0.542)	0.00459 (0.415)
Stock Concentration:		
0-5%	0.04269 (1.406)	0.03247 (1.118)
5-25%	0.03048 (2.738) *	0.02720 (2.557) **
Over 25%	-0.00162 (-0.248)	-0.00197 (-0.332)
Profit over Assets (log)	-0.20813 (-1.702) ***	-----
Market Value over Total Assets (log)	-----	-0.34421 (-3.687) *
R^2 (Adjusted)	30.56%	34.13%
F	9.996 *	12.284 *

concentration in one case, where compensation is deflated by total sales and performance is measured in terms of return on assets.

With regard to the signs of the coefficients, the diversification measures are found to be negatively related to the deflated measure of compensation, while the coefficients of both measures of ownership structure are positive in all equations. The coefficients on the firm performance variables are positive when the compensation variable is deflated by assets or market value, but negative when total sales is used as a deflator.

The Nonmonotonic Model with Size as an Independent Variable

The final stage of the regression analysis involves the inclusion of a company size variable as an independent variable in both the piecewise and strictly linear models. Size is measured as either total assets or total sales. The results of the piecewise linear regression, which again includes two alternative measures of firm performance, are presented in Table 5.7.

Table 5.5 (Continued)

Dependent Variable - Log (Compensation/Market Value)

Independent Variables	Regression # 1 [b]	Regression # 2 [c]
Related Diversification	-0.14492	-0.12335
	(-3.236) *	(-2.884) *
Unrelated	-0.15768	-0.11989
Diversification	(-2.936) *	(-2.351) **
Management		
Stockholdings:		
0-5%	0.16813	0.18997
	(4.352) *	(5.045) *
5-25%	-0.01681	-0.02799
	(-1.198)	(-2.227) **
Over 25%	0.00278	0.00416
	(0.243)	(0.378)
Stock Concentration:		
0-5%	0.05347	0.03501
	(1.793) **	(1.211)
5-25%	0.01642	0.02426
	(1.502)	(2.291) **
Over 25%	0.00516	0.00065
	(0.803)	(0.109)
Profit over Assets (log)	0.54883	-----
	(4.570) *	
Market Value over Total	-----	0.57208
Assets (log)		(6.155) *
R ^{2} (Adjusted)	35.15%	37.72%
F	12.080 *	14.189 *

[a]T-statistics are in parentheses. The significance levels are indicated as follows: *for $< .01$, **for $< .05$, and *** for $< .10$.

[b]Regression 1 is where performance is measured as the logarithm of profit over assets.

[c]Regression 2 is where performance is measured as the logarithm of market value over total assets.

In all four alternative equations, the size, diversification, and firm performance variables are significant. Furthermore, the signs of the coefficients are all positive, as expected. All four equations are significant and explain an adequate amount of the variance in the compensation variable.

With one exception, the ownership structure variables for the piecewise regressions are not significant. The one exception is in the case of management stockholdings of 0–5 percent, when size is measured as total assets and performance as the logarithm of profits over assets. In this case a significant negative relationship is found between management stockholdings of 0–5 percent and the logarithm of compensation. With these findings in mind, the analysis proceeds to test a strictly linear relationship in the case of management stockholdings and stock concentration.

Table 5.6
Results of Linear Regression Analysis[a]

Dependent Variable – Log (Compensation/Total Assets)		
Independent Variables	Regression # 1 [b]	Regression # 2 [c]
Related Diversification	-0.1868	-0.1578
	(-2.447) **	(-2.188) **
Unrelated Diversification	-0.2472	-0.2011
	(-3.179) *	(-2.730) *
Management Stockholdings	0.1488	0.1218
	(2.299) **	(1.952) ***
Stock Concentration	0.2800	0.2589
	(4.350) *	(4.175) *
Profit over Assets (log)	0.3211	____
	(4.812) *	____
Market Value over Total		
Assets (log)	____	0.3801
	____	(5.977) *
R^2 (adjusted)	28.70%	29.22%
F	15.811 *	17.187 *

The Strictly Linear Model with Size as an Independent Variable

Table 5.8 summarizes the results of the final four regression models. These linear regressions utilize the logarithm of compensation as the dependent variable, and company size (two alternative measurements), related diversification, unrelated diversification, management stockholdings, and firm performance (accounting and market measures) as independent variables. All four equations are significant and explain an adequate amount of the variance of compensation.

Company size (as measured by either total assets or total sales), related diversification, unrelated diversification, and firm performance (as measured by either profit over assets or market value over assets) are both positively and significantly related to compensation in all cases. Furthermore, stock concen-

Table 5.6 (Continued)

Dependent Variable - Log (Compensation/Total Sales)

Independent Variables	Regression # 1 [b]	Regression # 2[c]
Related Diversification	-0.1696	-0.1689
	(-2.045) **	(-2.188) **
Unrelated Diversification	-0.1851	-0.2154
	(-2.191) **	(-2.730) *
Management Stockholdings	0.1126	0.1304
	(1.600)	(1.952) ***
Stock Concentration	0.3279	0.2772
	(4.687) *	(4.175) *
Profit over Assets (log)	-0.1195	____
	(-1.648)	____
Market Value over Total		
Assets (log)	____	-0.2629
	____	(-3.860) *
R^2 (adjusted)	15.77%	18.86%
F	7.891 *	10.109 *

tration is both significant and negatively related to compensation in all four equations. In the case of management stockholdings, three of the four equations yield a significant negative relationship. The coefficient on management stock-holdings for the model that includes total sales as a size variable and performance measured as profit over assets is negative, but not significant at the 10 percent level.

PATH ANALYSIS MODELS

Path analysis is used to test the partial mediation models in Figures 5.1 and 5.2. Figure 5.1 does not include firm size as an independent variable, while Figure 5.2 does. Initial path coefficients are derived by regressing each variable on all prior variables in each model. In accordance with the theory-trimming approach to path analysis suggested by James, Mulaik, and Brett,[4] coefficients not significant at the 10 percent acceptance level or better are assumed to be zero.

Table 5.6 (Continued)

Dependent Variable - Log (Compensation/Market Value)

Independent Variables	Regression # 1 [b]	Regression # 2 [c]
Related Diversification	-0.2427	-0.2185
	(-3.144) *	(-2.984) *
Unrelated Diversification	-0.2251	-0.1786
	(-2.863) *	(-2.387) **
Management Stockholdings	0.1292	0.1051
	(1.974) ***	(1.658) ***
Stock Concentration	0.2989	0.2748
	(4.590) *	(4.363) *
Profit over Assets (log)	0.2883	____
	(4.272) *	____
Market Value over Total		
Assets (log)	____	0.3465
	____	(5.363) *
R^2 (adjusted)	27.05%	26.96%
F	14.647 *	15.466 *

[a]Standardized betas are reported. T statistics are in parentheses. The significance levels are indicated as follows: * for $< .01$, ** for $< .05$, and *** for $< .10$.

[b]Regression 1 is where performance is measured as the logarithm of profit over assets.

[c]Regression 2 is where performance is measured as the logarithm of market value over total assets.

Path Model 1 with Alternative Measures of Performance

The initial path coefficients for Model 1 with executive compensation defined as the log of compensation, and two alternative measures of firm performance, the log of profit over assets and the log of market value over assets, are presented in Table 5.9.

Mixed support is shown for the path model described in Figure 5.1. All paths emanating from diversification strategy to ownership structure are insignificant, whether performance is measured as the logarithm of profits over assets or the logarithm of market value over assets. Significant evidence is found for all other hypothesized paths, when performance is measured as the logarithm of profits over assets. The results of the analysis using the logarithm of market

Table 5.7
Results of Piecewise Regression Analysis[a]

With Size as Measured by Total Assets as an Independent Variable

Independent Variables	Regression # 1 [b]	Regression # 2 [c]
Total Assets	0.00001	0.00001
	(3.222) *	(3.267) *
Related Diversification	0.03933	0.05886
	(2.112) **	(2.990) *
Unrelated	0.06263	0.07021
Diversification	(2.776) *	(2.981) *
Management		
Stockholdings:		
0-5%	-0.03048	-0.01858
	(-1.818) ***	(-1.028)
5-25%	0.00312	-0.00724
	(0.545)	(-1.244)
Over 25%	-0.00319	0.00205
	(-0.669)	(0.404)
Stock Concentration:		
0-5%	-0.01022	-0.01683
	(-0.820)	(-1.265)
5-25%	-0.00394	-0.00193
	(-0.860)	(-0.394)
Over 25%	-0.00111	-0.00077
	(-0.412)	(-0.282)
Profit over Assets (log)	0.15187	-----
	(2.992) *	
Market Value over Total	-----	0.12288
Assets (log)		(2.782) *
R² (Adjusted)	18.30%	20.00%
F	5.121 *	5.899 *

value over assets are similar in sign, but insignificant for the paths between related diversification and performance, and stock concentration and performance.

The final estimates of the path coefficients after the insignificant paths have been excluded, for the model in which performance is measured as the logarithm of profits over assets, are reported in Figure 5.3. The decomposition of the causal relationships shown in Figure 5.3 are reported in Table 5.10. These results would be similar in the case where performance is measured by the logarithm of market value over assets except for the paths between related diversification and performance, and stock concentration and performance, which would be eliminated.

Figure 5.3 suggests that both ownership structure and diversification strategy affect executive compensation directly and indirectly through the mediator of firm performance, defined as the logarithm of profit over assets. Table 5.10 shows that 82.46 percent of the effect of stock concentration on executive compensation is direct, while 11.53% is mediated by firm performance and management stockholdings; 74.82 percent of the effect of management stockhold-

Table 5.7 (Continued)

With Size as Measured by Total Sales as an Independent Variable

Independent Variables	Regression # 1 [b]	Regression # 2 [c]
Total Sales	0.00001 (3.396) *	0.00001 (3.491) *
Related Diversification	0.03759 (2.014) **	0.05669 (2.890) *
Unrelated Diversification	0.06273 (2.791) *	0.07076 (3.018) *
Management Stockholdings:		
0-5%	-0.03129 (-1.886) ***	-0.01934 (-1.083)
5-25%	0.00315 (0.552)	-0.00726 (-1.253)
Over 25%	-0.00312 (-0.656)	0.00209 (0.414)
Stock Concentration:		
0-5%	-0.01049 (-0.845)	-0.01705 (-1.287)
5-25%	-0.00372 (-0.813)	-0.00163 (-0.334)
Over 25%	-0.00115 (-0.428)	-0.00082 (-0.303)
Profit over Assets (log)	0.15033 (2.978) *	-----
Market Value over Total Assets (log)	-----	0.12544 (2.850) *
R ^{2} (Adjusted)	18.81%	20.61%
F	5.262 *	6.088 *

Note: Size is measured by total assets as an independent variable.

[a]T statistics are in parentheses. The significance levels are indicated as follows: * for < .01, ** for < .05, and *** for < .10.

[b]Regression 1 is where performance is measured as the logarithm of profit over assets.

[c]Regression 2 is where performance is measured as the logarithm of market value over total assets.

ings on executive compensation is direct and 25.18 percent is mediated by firm performance; 83.81 percent of the effect of related diversification is direct and 16.18 percent is mediated by firm performance; and 80.25 percent of the effect of unrelated diversification is direct and 19.70 percent is mediated by firm performance.

Path Model 1 with Compensation Deflated by Size and Alternative Measures of Performance

In this part of the analysis, initial path coefficients are obtained for six versions of the model shown in Figure 5.1. The compensation variable is deflated by three measures of company size: total assets, total sales, and market value.

Table 5.8
Results of Linear Regression Analysis[a]

With Size as Measured by Total Assets as an Independent Variable

Independent Variables	Regression # 1 [b]	Regression # 2 [c]
Total Assets	0.27559	0.26471
	(3.925) *	(3.854) *
Related Diversification	0.17553	0.23331
	(2.146) **	(3.032) *
Unrelated Diversification	0.22952	0.23610
	(2.738) *	(2.989) *
Management Stockholdings	-0.09707	-0.14239
	(-1.392) ***	(-2.127) **
Stock Concentration	-0.15998	-0.13307
	(-2.281) **	(-1.979) **
Profit over Assets (log)	0.23161	_____
	(3.200) *	_____
Market Value over Total Assets (log)	_____	0.22019
	_____	(3.156) *
R^2 (adjusted)	18.11%	19.39%
F	7.781 *	8.859 *

Furthermore, performance is measured in terms of both profit over assets and market value over assets. The initial path coefficients for each of the six versions are presented in Table 5.11.

Table 5.11 shows that for all versions of the model in this section, the paths between diversification strategy and ownership structure are insignificant. Furthermore, when performance is measured as the logarithm of market value over assets, the initial path coefficients are insignificant for paths between related diversification and performance, regardless of the size variable utilized to deflate compensation. Also, the coefficient for the path between stock concentration and performance (as measured by the logarithm of market value over assets) is also insignificant, corresponding to previous results. Finally, the path between management stockholdings and performance, as measured by the logarithm of market value over assets, is not supported when compensation is deflated by total assets or market value.

Table 5.8 (Continued)

With Size as Measured by Total Sales as an Independent Variable

Independent Variables	Regression # 1 [b]	Regression # 2 [c]
Total Sales	0.28171	0.27490
	(4.045) *	(4.030) *
Related Diversification	0.16566	0.22357
	(2.029) **	(2.913) *
Unrelated Diversification	0.23063	0.23842
	(2.760) *	(3.032) *
Management Stockholdings	-0.09824	-0.14414
	(-1.413)	(-2.162) **
Stock Concentration	-0.15903	-0.13091
	(-2.274) **	(-1.953) ***
Profit over Assets (log)	0.22845	____
	(3.171) *	____
Market Value over Total		
Assets (log)	____	0.22341
	____	(3.211) *
R^2 (adjusted)	18.51%	19.94%
F	7.967 *	9.135 *

Note: Size is measured by total sales as an independent variable.

[a] Standardized betas are reported. T statistics are in parentheses. The significance levels are indicated as follows: * for $< .01$, ** for $< .05$, and *** for $< .10$.

[b] Regression 1 is where performance is measured as the logarithm of profit over assets.

[c] Regression 2 is where performance is measured as the logarithm of market value over total assets.

When performance is measured as the logarithm of profit over assets, all paths in Figure 5.3 are supported with two exceptions. When compensation is deflated by total assets or market value, the path between related diversification and performance (measured as the log of profits over assets) is not supported.

Path Model 2 with Size in the Model

The initial path coefficients for Model 2 with executive compensation defined as the log of compensation, two alternative measures of firm performance (the

Figure 5.1
Research Model 1

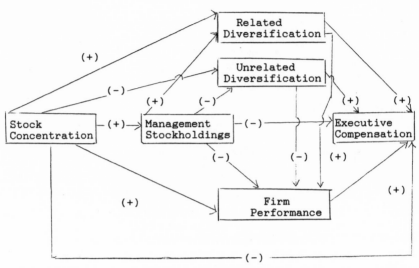

Note: The sign for each path corresponds with its expected or proposed sign. Size is not included as an independent variable.

Figure 5.2
Research Model 2

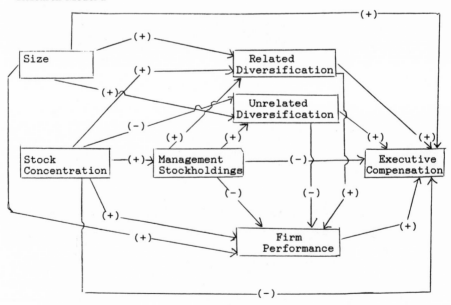

Note: The sign for each path corresponds with expected or proposed sign. Size is included as an independent variable.

Table 5.9
Initial Path Coefficients

Performance Defined as Log (Profit/Assets)

Variables	1	2	3	4	5
1. Related Diversification			-0.044	-0.118	
2. Unrelated Diversification			0.048	0.056	
3. Management Stockholdings				0.1433 **	
4. Stock Concentration					
5. Profit over Assets, logarithm	-0.1833***	-0.3471*	0.2263*	-0.1115***	
6. Executive Compensation, logarithm	0.1781***	0.2653**	-0.1248***	-0.2097*	0.1878***

Performance Defined as Log (Market Value/Assets)

Variables	1	2	3	4	5
1. Related Diversification			-0.076	-0.062	
2. Unrelated Diversification			0.046	-0.003	
3. Management Stockholdings				0.1433 **	
4. Stock Concentration					
5. Market Value over Assets, logarithm	-0.1077	-0.3247*	0.1921*	-0.0976	
6. Executive Compensation, logarithm	0.2367*	0.2658*	-0.1651***	-0.1793*	0.1577***

* p < 0.01
** p < 0.05
*** p < 0.10

123

Figure 5.3
Final Path Model and Coefficients

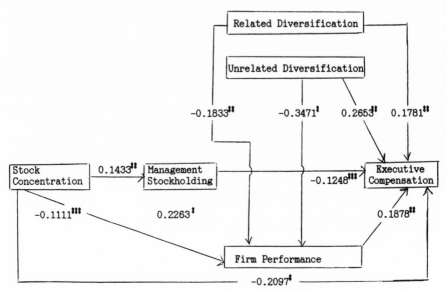

Note: These results correspond to the research model proposed in Figure 5.1, with executive compensation measured as the logarithm of compensation and firm performance measured as the logarithm of profit over assets.

  *p$<$0.01
 **p$<$0.05
***p$<$0.10

log of profit over assets and the log of market value over assets), and two alternative measures of firm size (total assets and total sales) are presented in Table 5.12.

Mixed support is shown for the path model described in Figure 5.2. All paths emanating from diversification strategy to ownership structure are insignificant for all four specifications of the model. However, significant evidence is found for all other hypothesized paths when performance is measured as the logarithm of profits over assets and size is measured as total assets. When size is measured as total sales, the results of the analysis for performance measured similarly are insignificant with regard to the path between management stockholdings and compensation, but significant for all others.

The results of the analysis using the logarithm of market value over assets are similar in sign, but insignificant for the paths between related diversification and performance, regardless of the measurement of size.

The final estimates of the path coefficients (after the insignificant paths have

Table 5.10
Decomposition Table for the Final Path Model Shown in Figure 5.3

Bivariate Relationships	Causal Path		
	Direct	Indirect	Total
1. Executive Compensation and Related Diversification	0.1781	(0.1833)(0.1878)=0.0344	0.2125
2. Executive Compensation and Unrelated Diversification	0.2653	(0.3471)(0.1878)=0.0651	0.3304
3. Executive Compensation and Firm Performance	0.1878		0.1878
4. Executive Compensation and Stock Concentration	-0.2097	(0.1111)(0.1878)+ (0.1433)(0.1248)+ (0.1433)(0.2263)(0.1878)= 0.0446	0.2543
5. Executive Compensation and Management Stockholdings	-0.1248	(0.2263)(0.1878)=0.042	0.1668
6. Firm Performance and Stock Concentration	-0.1111	(0.1433)(0.2263)=0.032	0.1431
7. Firm Performance and Related Diversification	-0.1833		0.1833
8. Firm Performance and and Unrelated Diversification	-0.3471		0.3471
9. Stock Concentration and Management Stockholdings	0.1433		0.1433
10. Firm Performance and Management Stockholdings	0.2263		0.2263

been excluded) for the model in which performance is measured as the logarithm of profits over assets and size is measured as total assets are reported in Figure 5.4. The decomposition of the causal relationships shown in Figure 5.4 is reported in Table 5.13. These results would be similar to the case in which

Table 5.11
Initial Path Coefficients

Compensation Deflated by Total Assets

Performance Defined as Log (Profit/Assets)

Variables	1	2	3	4	5
1. Related Diversification			-0.0387	-0.1062	
2. Unrelated Diversification			0.0544	0.0711	
3. Management Stockholdings				0.1433 **	
4. Stock Concentration					
5. Profit over Assets, logarithm	-0.0715	-0.1855***	0.1335****	-0.237*	
6. Executive Compensation over Total Assets, logarithm	-0.1868***	-0.2472*	0.1488**	0.2800*	0.321*

Performance Defined as Log (Market Value/Assets)

Variables	1	2	3	4	5
1. Related Diversification			-0.0862	-0.0639	
2. Unrelated Diversification			0.0391	0.0086	
3. Management Stockholdings				0.1433 **	
4. Stock Concentration					
5. Market Value over Assets, logarithm	0.0056	-0.1599****	0.0918	-0.2170*	
6. Executive Compensation over Total Assets, logarithm	-0.1578***	0.201*	0.1218***	0.2589*	0.380*

Compensation Deflated by Total Sales

Performance Defined as Log (Profit/Assets)

Variables	1	2	3	4	5
1. Related Diversification					
2. Unrelated Diversification					
3. Management Stockholdings	-0.0397	0.0386			
4. Stock Concentration	-0.0992	0.0513	0.1433 ***		
5. Profit over Assets, logarithm	-0.1749***	-0.3276*	0.2218***	-0.1116	
6. Executive Compensation over Total Sales, logarithm	-0.1696***	-0.1854***	0.1126	0.3279*	-0.1195

Performance Defined as Log (Market Value/Assets)

Variables	1	2	3	4	5
1. Related Diversification					
2. Unrelated Diversification					
3. Management Stockholdings	-0.0862	0.0391			
4. Stock Concentration	-0.0639	0.0086	0.1433 ***		
5. Market Value over Assets, logarithm	-0.1124	-0.3273*	0.1926*	-0.0444	
6. Executive Compensation over Total Sales, logarithm	-0.1689***	-0.2154*	0.1304****	0.2772*	-0.2629*

Table 5.11 (Continued)

Compensation Deflated by Market Value

Performance Defined as Log (Profit/Assets)

Variables	1	2	3	4	5
1. Related Diversification			-0.0281	-0.0763	
2. Unrelated Diversification			0.0417	0.0522	
3. Management Stockholdings				0.1433 **	
4. Stock Concentration					
5. Profit over Assets, logarithm	-0.0637	-0.2083***	0.1498**	-0.2365*	
6. Executive Compensation over Market Value, logarithm	-0.2427*	-0.2251*	0.1292***	0.2989**	0.2883*

Performance Defined as Log (Market Value/Assets)

Variables	1	2	3	4	5
1. Related Diversification			-0.0757	-0.0350	
2. Unrelated Diversification			0.0283	-0.0109	
3. Management Stockholdings				0.1433 **	
4. Stock Concentration					
5. Market Value over Assets, logarithm	0.0208	-0.1836***	0.1071	-0.2169*	
6. Executive Compensation over Market Value, logarithm	-0.2185*	-0.1786***	0.1051***	0.2748**	0.3465**

*p < 0.01
**p < 0.05
**p < 0.10

128

Table 5.12
Initial Path Coefficients

Size as Measured by Total Assets

Performance Defined as Log (Profit/Assets)

Variables	1	2	3	4	5	6
1. Related Diversification			-0.04950	-0.1278		-0.8433
2. Unrelated Diversification			0.05390	0.6579		0.0862
3. Management Stockholdings				0.1433***		
4. Stock Concentration						
5. Profit over Assets, logarithm	-0.18397***	-0.32083*	0.20307*	-0.13102***		-0.20626*
6. Total Assets						
7. CEO Compensation, logarithm	0.17553***	0.22952*	-0.09707***	-0.15998***	0.23161*	0.27559*

Performance Defined as Log (Market Value/Assets)

Variables	1	2	3	4	5	6
1. Related Diversification			-0.07592	-0.06169		
2. Unrelated Diversification			0.04565	-0.00354		
3. Management Stockholdings				0.1433***		
4. Stock Concentration						
5. Market Value over Assets, logarithm	-0.11384	-0.28890*	0.16213***	-0.12487***		-0.27704*
6. Total Assets						
7. CEO Compensation, logarithm	0.23331*	0.23610***	-0.14239***	-0.13307***	0.22019*	0.26471*

Table 5.12 (Continued)

Size as Measured by Total Sales

Performance Defined as Log (Profit/Assets)

Variables	1	2	3	4	5	6
1. Related Diversification			-0.04667	-0.1229		0.0052
2. Unrelated Diversification			0.05167	0.6229		0.0542
3. Management Stockholdings				0.1433***		
4. Stock Concentration						
5. Profit over Assets, logarithm	-0.17799***	-0.32513*	0.20652*	-0.12957***		-0.19359*
6. Total Sales						
7. CEO Compensation, logarithm	0.16566***	0.23063*	-0.09824	-0.15903***	0.22845*	0.28171*

Performance Defined as Log (Market Value/Assets)

Variables	1	2	3	4	5	6
1. Related Diversification			-0.07747	-0.06646		-0.38585
2. Unrelated Diversification			0.07201	0.00125		0.03880
3. Management Stockholdings				0.1433***		
4. Stock Concentration						
5. Market Value over Assets, logarithm	-0.10478	-0.29241*	0.16486***	-0.12488***		-0.28103*
6. Total Sales						
7. CEO Compensation, logarithm	0.22357*	0.23842*	-0.14414***	-0.13091***	0.22341*	0.27490*

$*p < 0.01$
$**p < 0.05$
$***p < 0.10$

Figure 5.4
Final Path Model and Coefficients

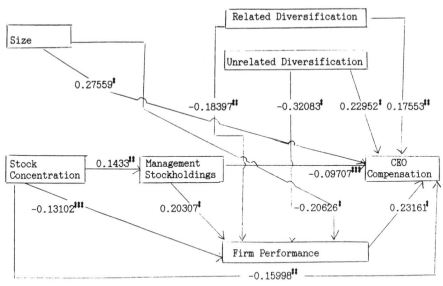

Note: These results correspond to the research model proposed in Figure 5.2, with executive compensation measured as the logarithm of compensation, firm performance measured as the logarithm of profit over assets, and size measured as total assets.

*p<0.01
**p<0.05
***p<0.10

performance is measured as the log of market value over assets except for the path between related diversification and performance, which would be eliminated.

Figure 5.4 suggests that ownership structure, firm size (measured as total assets), and diversification strategy affect executive compensation directly and indirectly through the mediator of firm performance (defined as the log of profit over assets). Table 5.13 shows that 75.84 percent of the effect of stock concentration on executive compensation is direct and 24.16 percent is mediated by firm performance and management stockholdings; 67.36 percent of the effect of management stockholdings on executive compensation is direct and 32.64 percent is mediated by firm performance; 80.47 percent of the effect of related diversification is direct and 19.53 percent is mediated by firm performance; 75.54 percent of the effect of unrelated diversification is direct and 24.46 percent is mediated by firm performance; and 85.23 percent of the effect of size (measured as total assets) is direct and 14.77 percent is mediated by firm performance.

Table 5.13

Decomposition Table for the Final Path Model Shown in Figure 5.4

	Causal Path		
Bivariate Relationships	Direct	Indirect	Total
1. CEO Compensation and Related Diversification	0.17553	(0.18397)(0.23161)=0.04261	0.21814
2. CEO Compensation and Unrelated Diversification	0.22952	(0.32083)(0.23161)=0.07431	0.30383
3. CEO Compensation and Firm Performance	0.23161		0.23161
4. CEO Compensation and Management Stockholdings	-0.09707	(0.20307)(0.23161)=0.04703	0.14410
5. CEO Compensation and Size	0.27559	(0.20626)(0.23161)=0.04777	0.32336
6. CEO Compensation and Stock Concentration	-0.15998	(0.1433)(0.09707)+(0.1433)(0.20307)(0.23161)+(0.13102)(0.23161)=0.05099	0.21097
7. Firm Performance and Related Diversification	-0.18397		0.18397
8. Firm Performance and Unrelated Diversification	-0.32083		0.32083
9. Firm Performance and Size	0.20626		0.20626
10. Firm Performance and Management Stockholdings	0.20307		0.20307
11. Firm Performance and Stock Concentration	0.13102	(0.1433)(0.20307)=0.02910	0.16012
12. Stock Concentration and Management Stockholdings	0.1433		0.1433

NOTES

1. See J. Neter and W. Wasserman, *Applied Linear Statistical Models* (Homewood, Ill.: Irwin, 1974).

2. R. A. Morck, A. Shleifer, and R. W. Vishny, "Management Ownership and Market Valuation," *Journal of Financial Economics* 20 (1988): 293–315.

3. H. Demsetz and K. Lehn, "The Structure of Corporate Ownership: Theory and Consequences," *Journal of Political Economy* 93 (1985): 1155–77.

4. L. R. James, S. A. Mulaik, and J. M. Brett, *Causal Analysis, Assumptions, Models and Data* (Beverly Hills, Calif.: Sage, 1982).

Appendix
1987 Cash Compensation, Age, and Tenure Data for CEOs

COMPANY	CASH COMPENSATION 1987 (In thousands)	AGE OF CEO	YEARS WITH COMPANY	YEARS AS CEO
BOEING	737	56	31	2
LOCKHEED	832	64	31	3
MARTIN MARIETTA	680	52	12	0.83
MCDONNELL DOUGLAS	570	49	27	0.58
MAYTAG	872	61	37	15
WHIRPOOL	465	45	21	1
CHRYSLER	650	63	10	9
DANA	661	60	45	9
ECHLIN	504	61	26	19
FEDERAL-MOGUL	861	63	47	13
GENERAL MOTORS	1667	62	40	8
MACK TRUCKS	370	53	22	5
PACCAR	769	58	33	22
STANDARD PRODUCTS	389	61	33	27
ANHEUSER-BUSCH	1455	50	32	13
BROWN-FORMAN	928	51	29	14
COORS (ADOLPH)	365	42	21	3
GENERAL CINEMA	723	63	43	28
PEPSICO	1134	52	22	2
LONE STAR INDUSTRIES	500	65	18	16
MASCO	1025	51	4	4
OWENS-CORNING FIBERGLASS	1000	62	39	16
SHERWIN-WILLIAMS	839	53	11	10
USG	833	62	39	3
AIR PRODUCTS & CHEMICALS	854	60	37	2
AMERICAN CYANAMID	1411	59	35	6
DEXTER	510	62	42	30
DOW CHEMICAL	907	52	30	0.83
ECOLAB	619	60	6	6
ENGLEHARD	890	52	12	4
ETHYL	726	65	46	19
FERRO	490	61	42	12
FREEPORT-MCMORAN	926	49	22	4
GAF	736	48	5	5
GRACE (W. R.)	1200	74	53	43
LUBRIZOL	649	57	34	10
MONSANTO	925	53	27	6
MORTON THIOKOL	930	58	14	9
NALCO CHEMICAL	700	55	29	6
OLIN	648	55	10	1
PENNWALT	444	60	38	10

Appendix (Continued)

COMPANY	CASH COMPENSATION 1987 (In thousands)	AGE OF CEO	YEARS WITH COMPANY	YEARS AS CEO
ROHM & HAAS	636	51	24	0.25
UNION CARBIDE	1000	55	34	3
WITCO	550	63	39	18
ALLIED-SIGNAL	1380	59	9	9
FIGGIE INTERNATIONAL	1328	64	25	25
IC INDUSTRIES	650	54	1	1
ITT	1887	56	23	9
ROCKWELL INTERNATIONAL	1108	49	21	0.67
TELEDYNE	800	68	23	3
TENNECO	1049	57	30	11
BALL	500	61	19	8
ABBOTT LABS	1329	59	16	9
AMERICAN HOME PRODUCTS	1310	50	19	2
BARD (C. R.)	815	60	13	13
BAXTER TRAVENOL LABS	1202	53	23	8
BECTON DICKINSON	1298	66	40	9
BRISTOL-MEYERS	1297	63	39	17
JOHNSON & JOHNSON	1282	62	36	13
LILLY (ELI)	1009	61	39	16
MARION LABS	876	52	19	5
MERCK	1372	58	14	3
PFIZER	1249	60	25	17
SCHERING-PLOUGH	1221	54	11	7
SMITHKLINE BECKMAN	1529	54	34	7
SQUIBB	1405	64	34	21
UPJOHN	803	59	9	1
WARNER-LAMBERT	1155	61	39	4
AMETEK	600	69	23	19
AMP	541	63	36	6
CHAMPION SPARK PLUG	443	50	2	2
COMBUSTION ENGINEERING	933	59	7	4
GENERAL INSTRUMENT	798	60	25	15
HARRIS	733	57	33	2
LITTON INDUSTRIES	783	59	32	2
MEDTRONIC	569	61	3	3
AMERICAN BRANDS	985	58	10	1
PHILIP MORRIS	1494	61	35	4
UST	1535	59	27	16
COOPER TIRE & RUBBER	389	62	39	11
GOODYEAR TIRE & RUBBER	1252	63	42	8
MOTOROLA	488	47	13	0.75
RAYTHEON	1005	63	41	20

Appendix (Continued)

COMPANY	CASH COMPENSATION 1987 (In thousands)	AGE OF CEO	YEARS WITH COMPANY	YEARS AS CEO
SQUARE D	822	59	8	5
TRW	1061	63	34	11
TEXAS INSTRUMENT	685	50	30	3
WESTINGHOUSE ELECTRIC	980	62	40	0.75
ARCHER DANIELS MIDLAND	1104	69	23	18
BORDEN	1004	63	26	2
CAMPBELL SOUP	696	61	33	8
CPC INTERNATIONAL	870	60	26	4
CONAGRA	1312	60	15	14
DEAN FOODS	551	50	34	1
GENERAL MILLS	1310	56	31	7
GERBER PRODUCTS	651	55	1	1
HEINZ (H. J.)	1099	51	20	9
HERSHEY FOODS	660	55	31	5
HORMEL (GEO. A.)	799	55	35	7
INTERNATIONAL MULTIFOODS	760	61	38	4
KELLOGG	1100	61	39	10
KRAFT	1200	60	35	9
MCCORMICK	436	59	40	2
QUAKER OATS	998	49	23	7
RALSTON PURINA	869	53	25	7
SARA LEE	1301	51	21	13
TYSON FOODS	3445	57	39	22
UNIVERSAL FOODS	576	60	34	10
WRIGLEY (WM. JR.)	556	54	33	28
CINCINNATI MILICRON	1509	62	38	12
INGERSOLL-RAND	1043	64	38	8
INTERLAKE	649	60	10	7
SUNDSTRAND	700	61	37	9
FOXBORO	221	42	14	0.75
JOHNSON CONTROLS	482	47	23	0.75
PERKIN ELMER	395	59	37	4
TEKTRONIX	356	48	15	0.92
AMERICAN GREETINGS	375	47	28	1
BRUNSWICK	1155	57	31	6
EASTMAN KODAK	1044	62	39	5
FLEETWOOD ENTERPRISES	613	62	39	39
HASBRO	990	45	26	9
MATTEL	477	55	9	2
OUTBOARD MARINE	859	66	23	9
POLAROID	449	56	31	4
ALCOA	564	52	1	1

Appendix (Continued)

COMPANY	CASH COMPENSATION 1987 (In thousands)	AGE OF CEO	YEARS WITH COMPANY	YEARS AS CEO
NEWMONT MINING	938	52	30	3
BASSETT FURNITURE INDUSTRIES	382	60	32	10
BEMIS	831	62	24	11
BLACK & DECKER	711	44	4	3
HARTMARX	427	50	20	2
INTERCO	712	49	29	6
SHAW INDUSTRIES	723	56	28	20
SPRING INDUSTRIES	1000	55	9	8
VF	1075	54	9	7
WORTHINGTON INDUSTRIES	514	64	34	34
COOPER INDUSTRIES	880	56	28	13
DOVER	783	51	18	8
FMC	937	61	37	17
DELUXE CHECK PRINTERS	455	57	35	2
DONNELLY (R. R.) & SONS	659	53	24	5
COMMERCE CLEARING HOUSE	365	59	36	9
DOW JONES	700	61	42	14
GANNETT	1075	49	20	2
HARCOURT BRACE JOVANOVICH	1221	67	42	35
KNIGHT-RIDDER	688	51	32	0.5
MACMILLAN	704	45	10	9
MEDIA GENERAL	510	66	16	4
MEREDITH	713	60	37	12
NEW YORK TIMES	721	61	38	15
TIME, INC.	1288	56	32	8
TIMES MIRROR	1302	57	28	8
TRIBUNE CO.	922	62	38	14
WASHINGTON POST	684	70	26	15
CORNING GLASS WORKS	804	51	27	5
CRANE	826	43	15	6
AMOCO	1000	61	41	5
ASHLAND OIL	870	55	32	7
CHEVRON	874	64	41	7
EXXON	1207	59	37	2
KERR-MCGEE	467	54	32	0.42
MAPCO	672	53	6	5
MOBIL	1290	58	37	4
MURPHEY OIL	244	53	32	0.75
NERCO	418	50	12	12
SUN	852	59	24	3
TEXACO	723	59	35	2
UNOCAL	589	59	38	0.25

Appendix (Continued)

COMPANY	CASH COMPENSATION 1987 (In thousands)	AGE OF CEO	YEARS WITH COMPANY	YEARS AS CEO
AVON PRODUCTS	791	54	25	0.08
COLGATE-PALMOLIVE	664	59	39	3
GILLETTE	900	58	32	13
INT´L FLAVORS & FRAGRANCES	528	58	29	3
PROCTOR & GAMBLE	1300	60	37	8
TAMBRANDS	528	60	8	7
BOISE CASCADE	787	57	32	16
BOWATER	649	53	34	6
CHAMPION INTERNATIONAL	1139	56	32	15
CHESAPEAKE	509	48	30	8
CONSOLIDATED PAPERS	370	60	37	23
FEDERAL PAPER BOARD	1103	57	37	20
FORT HOWARD	776	52	25	4
GEORGIA-PACIFIC	900	61	14	5
GREAT NORTHERN NEKOOSA	590	60	39	4
INTERNATIONAL PAPER	926	56	10	4
JAMES RIVER CO. OF VIRGINIA	920	60	19	19
JEFFERSON SMURFIT	630	51	34	12
KIMBERLY-CLARK	1097	61	31	17
LOUISIANA PACIFIC	625	62	22	15
MEAD	1053	60	23	7
POTLATCH	865	58	18	18
SCOTT PAPER	802	52	30	7
SONOCO	642	54	31	19
STONE CONTAINER	757	52	32	10
TEMPLE-INLAND	665	53	21	6
UNION CAMP	662	58	23	3
WESTVACO	563	62	40	0.25
WEYERHAUSER	925	61	42	22
WILLAMETTE INDUSTRIES	425	57	36	9
CAMERON IRON WORKS	285	44	18	3
DRESSER INDUSTRIES	497	56	37	5
AMDAHL	898	52	12	5
APPLE COMPUTER	2140	48	5	5
COMPAQ COMPUTER	1375	42	7	7
DATA GENERAL	421	49	21	21
DIGITAL EQUIPMENT	906	61	31	31
HEWLETT-PACKARD	1046	55	31	10
INTERGRAPH	178	54	20	20
IBM	841	53	29	4
NCR	1001	58	13	5
PITNEY-BOWES	794	56	32	6

Appendix (Continued)

COMPANY	CASH COMPENSATION 1987 (In thousands)	AGE OF CEO	YEARS WITH COMPANY	YEARS AS CEO
PRIME COMPUTER	738	54	7	7
SEAGATE TECHNOLOGY	1264	57	10	10
STANDARD REGISTER	829	58	15	5
TANDEM COMPUTERS	513	47	15	15
UNISYS	1278	61	10	9
WANG LABORATORIES	393	67	38	38
XEROX	1138	57	18	6

**1987 Sales, Total Assets, Market Value, and Profit
(in millions)**

COMPANY	SALES	ASSETS	MARKET VALUE	PROFIT
BOEING	15355	12566	7423.6	480
LOCKHEED	11370	6301	2677.2	421
MARTIN MARIETTA	5165.1	2794.1	2423.7	230.6
MCDONNELL DOUGLAS	13146.1	2414.9	2414.9	313
MAYTAG	1908.8	854.9	17797.6	152.7
WHIRPOOL	4179	4423.7	1930.1	191.9
CHRYSLER	26257.7	19944.6	5353.9	1289.7
DANA	4142.1	2802	1549.7	144.4
ECHLIN	1099.7	869.1	868.8	152.7
FEDERAL-MOGUL	1075.4	803.6	517.9	41.1
GENERAL MOTORS	101781.9	87421.9	22314.9	3550.9
MACK TRUCKS	1857.7	1011.1	447.1	4.1
PACCAR	2423.5	1300	1255.7	112.5
STANDARD PRODUCTS	464.9	226	296	31.5
ANHEUSER-BUSCH	8258.4	6491.6	10419.9	614.7
BROWN-FORMAN	1098.1	1056.7	1500.3	89.6
COORS (ADOLPH)	1350.7	1456.5	736.5	48.1
GENERAL CINEMA	1052.9	1647.4	1288.9	69.4
PEPSICO	11500.2	9022.7	9147	594.8
LONE STAR INDUSTRIES	760.8	1492.8	491	57.2
MASCO	2023.3	2850.1	3447.3	218.8
OWENS-CORNING FIBERGLASS	2891.1	1590.1	804.8	200.1
SHERWIN-WILLIAMS	2094.8	1140	1251.6	96.6
USG	3046.4	2094.8	1855.2	204.3
AIR PRODUCTS & CHEMICALS	2140.4	2701.7	2529.6	155.6
AMERICAN CYANAMID	4166.1	4129	4559.4	275.6
DEXTER	782.8	451.9	636	42.8
DOW CHEMICAL	13377	14356	16026.3	1240
ECOLAB	989.3	982.4	734.6	52.2
ENGLEHARD	2479.2	1216.3	836.6	69.8
ETHYL	1720.3	1981	2596.4	193.3
FERRO	871.1	532	386.3	31.7
FREEPORT-MCMORAN	1514.4	3155.1	1839.2	248.8
GAF	836.9	1297.8	1476.4	237.6
GRACE (W. R.)	5046.3	4473.6	2310.8	173.1
LUBRIZOL	1013.4	939.4	1475.6	81.3
MONSANTO	7639	8455	5900.8	436
MORTON THIOKOL	1987.3	1666	2147.9	138
NALCO CHEMICAL	841.9	746.9	1468.1	80.3
OLIN	1930	1685	1135.9	78
PENNWALT	1196.8	781.9	604.6	52.4
ROHM & HAAS	2203	1954	2235.6	195.5
UNION CARBIDE	6914	7892	3244.3	232
WITCO	1427.6	1056.3	804.4	63.3

Appendix (Continued)

COMPANY	SALES	ASSETS	MARKET VALUE	PROFIT
ALLIED-SIGNAL	11597	10226	4798.4	656
FIGGIE INTERNATIONAL	1022.7	664.1	515.5	49.3
IC INDUSTRIES	4581.2	4871.4	33753.1	251.7
ITT	8551	13354.3	6316.3	1018.1
ROCKWELL INTERNATIONAL	12123.4	8739.2	55289.2	635.1
TELEDYNE	3216.8	3135	3888.4	377.2
TENNECO	15075	18503	6598.8	-218
BALL	1054.1	794.9	801.4	66.3
ABBOTT LABS	4387.9	4385.7	11024.8	632.6
AMERICAN HOME PRODUCTS	5028.3	4473.6	11617.6	845.1
BARD (C. R.)	641.3	487.6	1105.3	62.3
BAXTER TRAVENOL LABS	6223	7638	6000	331
BECTON DICKINSON	1582	1891.5	2482.5	148.2
BRISTOL-MEYERS	5401.2	4732	12584	709.6
JOHNSON & JOHNSON	8012	6546	14477.6	833
LILLY (ELI)	4049.3	5254.9	11254	643.7
MARION LABS	597.4	453.7	3388.1	96.9
MERCK	5061.3	5680	20783.3	906.4
PFIZER	4919.8	6922.6	8936.2	690.2
SCHERING-PLOUGH	2699.3	3179.5	5931.4	316.4
SMITHKLINE BECKMAN	4328.8	4446.2	7354	570.1
SQUIBB	2156.5	2782.4	6929	358.4
UPJOHN	2521	3043.1	5986	305
WARNER-LAMBERT	3484.7	2475.9	4904	295.8
AMETEK	620.1	538.4	724.8	41.2
AMP	2317.8	2082.1	5526.2	249.7
CHAMPION SPARK PLUG	995.6	653	460	19.1
COMBUSTION ENGINEERING	3301	2703.7	1331.6	56.6
GENERAL INSTRUMENT	947.2	940.3	1136.7	-80.4
HARRIS	2079	1796.4	1180.7	84.5
LITTON INDUSTRIES	4419.7	4880.8	2172.8	138.1
MEDTRONIC	502	559.7	1278	73.8
AMERICAN BRANDS	6323.4	7343.1	5009	522.7
PHILIP MORRIS	22279	19145	21998.4	1842
UST	564.5	549	1690	130.9
COOPER TIRE & RUBBER	665.8	413.3	347.2	30.7
GOODYEAR TIRE & RUBBER	10123.2	8395.9	3574.2	770.9
MOTOROLA	6707	5321	6141	308
RAYTHEON	7659.4	4062.2	4561.2	445.1
SQUARE D	1484.2	1193.1	1491.3	110
TRW	6821.2	4377.5	3033.4	243.4
TEXAS INSTRUMENT	5594.5	4256.3	4265	308.5
WESTINGHOUSE ELECTRIC	10679	9953.1	7231.2	738.9
ARCHER DANIELS MIDLAND	5774.6	3862.1	3509.7	265.4
BORDEN	6514.4	4157.4	3997.7	267.1

Appendix (Continued)

COMPANY	SALES	ASSETS	MARKET VALUE	PROFIT
CAMPBELL SOUP	4490.4	3090	3656.4	247.3
CPC INTERNATIONAL	4903	3260.5	3784.1	354.8
CONAGRA	9001.6	2482.5	1947.6	148.7
DEAN FOODS	1434.6	450.1	800.9	41.1
GENERAL MILLS	5208.3	2280.4	4422.6	222
GERBER PRODUCTS	1045.8	716.8	835.9	28.5
HEINZ (H. J.)	4639.5	3364.2	5456.8	338.5
HERSHEY FOODS	2433.8	1645.2	2423.8	148.2
HORMEL (GEO. A.)	2314.1	698	970.3	45.9
INTERNATIONAL MULTIFOODS	1533.4	644.7	456.6	51.5
KELLOGG	3793	2681	6236.8	-18.4
KRAFT	11010.5	5486.7	7178.2	489.4
MCCORMICK	1078.5	718	498.8	30.6
QUAKER OATS	4538.6	3250.1	3675.3	243.9
RALSTON PURINA	5868	3863.7	5173.9	523.1
SARA LEE	9154.6	4191.7	4636.6	267.1
TYSON FOODS	1786	806.8	890.3	67.8
UNIVERSAL FOODS	709.9	391.7	361.6	24.8
WRIGLEY (WM. JR.)	781.1	407.3	1582.9	70.1
CINCINNATI MILICRON	828	706.5	581.8	-80
INGERSOLL-RAND	2647.9	2248.2	2049.3	117.7
INTERLAKE	823.1	693.8	477.4	54.4
SUNDSTRAND	1365.5	1480.2	969.2	34.6
FOXBORO	504.4	428.1	360.2	-96.9
JOHNSON CONTROLS	2676.8	1739.1	1233.1	89.6
PERKIN ELMER	1333.6	1399.8	1235.8	-18.2
TEKTRONIX	1395.9	1159.4	790.4	51.2
AMERICAN GREETINGS	1102.5	1022.6	571.6	63.4
BRUNSWICK	3086.4	1896.3	1877	168.8
EASTMAN KODAK	13305	14451	13936.3	1178
FLEETWOOD ENTERPRISES	1259.3	482.2	478.1	39.7
HASBRO	1326.1	1076	753.2	48.2
MATTEL	1020.1	774.6	280.6	-113.2
OUTBOARD MARINE	1289.2	966.4	551.3	61.8
POALROID	1763.9	1624.9	2074.3	116.1
ALCOA	7767	9901.9	3966.9	200.1
NEWMONT MINING	558.5	1964.3	2339.1	340.9
BASSETT FURNITURE INDUSTRIES	475	286.9	289.8	22.3
BEMIS	930	545.3	492.8	32
BLACK & DECKER	1934.8	1668	1074.8	55.6
HARTMARX	1080.4	660.3	524.2	41.3
INTERCO	2613.7	1720.7	1554	98.6
SHAW INDUSTRIES	694.2	362.8	298.2	28.5
SPRING INDUSTRIES	1661.1	1083.7	555.5	55.7
VF	2573.8	1925.7	2188	179.7

Appendix (Continued)

COMPANY	SALES	ASSETS	MARKET VALUE	PROFIT
WORTHINGTON INDUSTRIES	818.8	455.2	868.4	42.1
COOPER INDUSTRIES	3585.8	3880.4	2903.4	173.8
DOVER	1585.5	1150.2	2053.9	111.7
FMC	3139.1	2595.1	996	180.5
DELUXE CHECK PRINTERS	948	866.3	2290.9	148.5
DONNELLY (R. R.) & SONS	2482.9	2086.4	2779.9	218.2
COMMERCE CLEARING HOUSE	551.5	522.2	1154.4	52.8
DOW JONES	1314.4	1942.6	3226.3	203
GANNETT	3079.4	3510.3	6053.5	319.4
HARCOURT BRACE JOVANOVICH	1291.4	2039.1	480.8	90.5
KNIGHT-RIDDER	2072.6	1985.4	2424.5	155.2
MACMILLAN	955.8	937.1	1500	70.7
MEDIA GENERAL	715.3	829.3	1322.4	42.9
MEREDITH	598.7	565.7	535.7	33.9
NEW YORK TIMES	1689.6	1711.6	2531.6	160.3
TIME, INC.	4193.5	4423.7	5267.2	249.8
TIMES MIRROR	3154.6	3122.1	4788.5	266.5
TRIBUNE CO.	2160	2758.4	3129.3	141.5
WASHINGTON POST	1315.4	1194.2	2443	186.7
CORNING GLASS WORKS	2083.7	2658.7	2438.1	207.5
CRANE	1284	661.7	678.9	59.3
AMOCO	20174	24827	19322.6	1360
ASHLAND OIL	6870.9	4058	1905.1	133.4
CHEVRON	26015	34465	15779.8	1007
EXXON	76416	74042	58074.5	4840
KERR-MCGEE	2608	3071	1749.1	81
MAPCO	1580.9	1365.4	1048.1	108.4
MOBIL	51223	41140	17842.7	1258
MURPHEY OIL	1474	2066.6	944	-43.6
NERCO	632.3	977.1	500.3	60.1
SUN	8691	12580	6037.8	348
TEXACO	34372	33962	10869.8	-4407
UNOCAL	8466	10062	4255.4	181
AVON PRODUCTS	3292.7	2559.2	1663.6	159.1
COLGATE-PALMOLIVE	1126	933.3	1700.9	104.9
GILLETTE	3166.8	2731.2	4503.7	229.9
INT'L FLAVORS & FRAGRANCES	745.9	874.6	1882.5	107
PROCTOR & GAMBLE	17000	13715	13691.4	327
TAMBRANDS	538.9	408.2	1251.9	76.6
BOISE CASCADE	3820.8	3374.8	2143.2	183
BOWATER	1231	1699.8	1281.9	81.1
CHAMPION INTERNATIONAL	4614.7	6103.3	3405.9	382
CHESAPEAKE	675.7	590.7	408.7	30.2
CONSOLIDATED PAPERS	742.8	804.4	1503.6	95.8
FEDERAL PAPER BOARD	1025.7	1183.5	794.9	65.8

Appendix (Continued)

COMPANY	SALES	ASSETS	MARKET VALUE	PROFIT
FORT HOWARD	1757.7	2196.2	2689	157.7
GEORGIA-PACIFIC	8603	5870	3888.4	458
GREAT NORTHERN NEKOOSA	2589	3538.5	2401.2	200.6
INTERNATIONAL PAPER	7763	8710	4518.4	407
JAMES RIVER CO. OF VIRGINIA	4479	4210.5	2037.2	169.9
JEFFERSON SMURFIT	1009.5	691.4	1064.6	92
KIMBERLY-CLARK	4884.7	3885.7	4601.5	325.2
LOUISIANA PACIFIC	1921.6	1971	1088.3	125
MEAD	4208.8	2917.3	2465.1	217.7
POTLATCH	992.1	1306.6	839.3	87.6
SCOTT PAPER	4122	4480.5	2692.6	233.8
SONOCO	1312.1	877.6	1096.6	61.5
STONE CONTAINER	3232.9	2286.1	1753.4	161.3
TEMPLE-INLAND	1602.7	1798	1279.7	141.4
UNION CAMP	2307.6	2896.1	2519	207.5
WESTVACO	1903.6	2214	1932.8	146.2
WEYERHAUSER	6989.8	7201.9	3244.3	446.6
WILLAMETTE INDUSTRIES	1431.6	1180.6	1149.7	121.3
CAMERON IRON WORKS	485	754.4	530.9	-110.2
DRESSER INDUSTRIES	3119.7	2882.3	2208.1	48.9
AMDAHL	1505.2	1507.5	1886.6	146
APPLE COMPUTER	2661.1	1477.9	5674	217.5
COMPAQ COMPUTER	1224.1	901	1799.5	136.3
DATA GENERAL	1274.3	1069.2	686.3	-127.1
DIGITAL EQUIPMENT	9389.4	8407.4	15113.4	1137.4
HEWLETT-PACKARD	8090	8133	16054.6	644
INTERGRAPH	641.1	704	1557.5	69.9
IBM	54217	63688	68063.9	5258
NCR	5640.7	4187.5	5593.8	419.3
PITNEY-BOWES	2250.5	2431.7	3379.1	199.4
PRIME COMPUTER	960.9	1334.6	794.7	64.8
SEAGATE TECHNOLOGY	958.1	814.1	1054.9	139.7
STANDARD REGISTER	659.7	452.2	715.5	40.5
TANDEM COMPUTERS	1035.5	967.2	1944.7	105.6
UNISYS	9712.9	9958	5248	578
WANG LABORATORIES	2836.7	2812	2093.7	-70.7
XEROX	10320	11598	5655.4	578

1987 SIC-Based Product Count Measures of Diversification

COMPANY	DIVERSIFICATION	
	RELATED	UNRELATED
BOEING	3	3
LOCKHEED	4	3
MARTIN MARIETTA	2	3
MCDONNELL DOUGLAS	4	2
MAYTAG	4	1
WHIRPOOL	5	1
CHRYSLER	3	2
DANA	1	2
ECHLIN	1	2
FEDERAL-MOGUL	1	4
GENERAL MOTORS	3	2
MACK TRUCKS	3	3
PACCAR	1	2
STANDARD PRODUCTS	3	0
ANHEUSER-BUSCH	5	1
BROWN-FORMAN	1	4
COORS (ADOLPH)	1	5
GENERAL CINEMA	1	3
PEPSICO	3	1
LONE STAR INDUSTRIES	3	2
MASCO	2	4
OWENS-CORNING FIBERGLASS	2	3
SHERWIN-WILLIAMS	4	1
USG	3	2
AIR PRODUCTS & CHEMICALS	4	1
AMERICAN CYANAMID	5	0
DEXTER	1	2
DOW CHEMICAL	6	0
ECOLAB	3	2
ENGLEHARD	2	1
ETHYL	3	2
FERRO	2	1
FREEPORT-MCMORAN	1	2
GAF	2	4
GRACE (W. R.)	1	4
LUBRIZOL	2	2
MONSANTO	6	0
MORTON THIOKOL	1	3
NALCO CHEMICAL	3	3
OLIN	3	3
PENNWALT	5	1
ROHM & HAAS	4	2
UNION CARBIDE	3	2
WITCO	1	2
ALLIED-SIGNAL	1	3

Appendix (Continued)

COMPANY	DIVERSIFICATION	
	RELATED	UNRELATED
FIGGIE INTERNATIONAL	3	3
IC INDUSTRIES	1	5
ITT	2	3
ROCKWELL INTERNATIONAL	4	2
TELEDYNE	1	6
TENNECO	1	3
BALL	1	3
ABBOTT LABS	3	3
AMERICAN HOME PRODUCTS	2	2
BARD (C. R.)	2	2
BAXTER TRAVENOL LABS	2	2
BECTON DICKINSON	2	3
BRISTOL-MEYERS	3	1
JOHNSON & JOHNSON	2	3
LILLY (ELI)	4	2
MARION LABS	1	1
MERCK	5	1
PFIZER	2	3
SCHERING-PLOUGH	2	1
SMITHKLINE BECKMAN	2	2
SQUIBB	1	2
UPJOHN	6	0
WARNER-LAMBERT	3	1
AMETEK	3	2
AMP	2	1
CHAMPION SPARK PLUG	1	4
COMBUSTION ENGINEERING	4	2
GENERAL INSTRUMENT	2	1
HARRIS	2	1
LITTON INDUSTRIES	2	3
MEDTRONIC	1	1
AMERICAN BRANDS	2	3
PHILIP MORRIS	1	2
UST	3	1
COOPER TIRE & RUBBER	2	0
GOODYEAR TIRE & RUBBER	3	2
MOTOROLA	5	1
RAYTHEON	3	3
SQUARE D	5	1
TRW	1	2
TEXAS INSTRUMENT	4	2
WESTINGHOUSE ELECTRIC	1	3
ARCHER DANIELS MIDLAND	5	0
BORDEN	6	0
CAMPBELL SOUP	5	1
CPC INTERNATIONAL	6	0

Appendix (Continued)

COMPANY	DIVERSIFICATION	
	RELATED	UNRELATED
CONAGRA	4	2
DEAN FOODS	5	0
GENERAL MILLS	5	1
GERBER PRODUCTS	1	4
HEINZ (H. J.)	6	0
HERSHEY FOODS	3	1
HORMEL (GEO. A.)	2	1
INTERNATIONAL MULTIFOODS	5	1
KELLOGG	5	0
KRAFT	4	2
MCCORMICK	4	1
QUAKER OATS	3	2
RALSTON PURINA	5	1
SARA LEE	3	3
TYSON FOODS	5	1
UNIVERSAL FOODS	4	1
WRIGLEY (WM. JR.)	1	0
CINCINNATI MILICRON	3	3
INGERSOLL-RAND	5	1
INTERLAKE	1	2
SUNDSTRAND	1	2
FOXBORO	1	2
JOHNSON CONTROLS	1	4
PERKIN ELMER	2	2
TEKTRONIX	1	1
AMERICAN GREETINGS	1	3
BRUNSWICK	1	4
EASTMAN KODAK	1	3
FLEETWOOD ENTERPRISES	1	2
HASBRO	2	1
MATTEL	2	0
OUTBOARD MARINE	2	1
POALROID	3	0
ALCOA	1	2
NEWMONT MINING	1	3
BASSETT FURNITURE INDUSTRIES	3	0
BEMIS	2	4
BLACK & DECKER	4	2
HARTMARX	3	1
INTERCO	1	4
SHAW INDUSTRIES	1	0
SPRING INDUSTRIES	4	1
VF	4	1
WORTHINGTON INDUSTRIES	2	2
COOPER INDUSTRIES	4	1
DOVER	1	2

Appendix (Continued)

COMPANY	DIVERSIFICATION	
	RELATED	UNRELATED
FMC	1	4
DELUXE CHECK PRINTERS	2	0
DONNELLY (R. R.) & SONS	3	0
COMMERCE CLEARING HOUSE	2	1
DOW JONES	3	2
GANNETT	1	2
HARCOURT BRACE JOVANOVICH	3	3
KNIGHT-RIDDER	1	4
MACMILLAN	1	1
MEDIA GENERAL	1	2
MEREDITH	2	3
NEW YORK TIMES	2	2
TIME, INC.	2	2
TIMES MIRROR	4	1
TRIBUNE CO.	1	3
WASHINGTON POST	3	1
CORNING GLASS WORKS	3	2
CRANE	2	2
AMOCO	1	3
ASHLAND OIL	2	4
CHEVRON	1	5
EXXON	1	3
KERR-MCGEE	2	3
MAPCO	1	5
MOBIL	2	3
MURPHEY OIL	1	4
NERCO	1	1
SUN	1	5
TEXACO	2	3
UNOCAL	1	4
AVON PRODUCTS	2	4
COLGATE-PALMOLIVE	2	3
GILLETTE	1	4
INT'L FLAVORS & FRAGRANCES	5	1
PROCTOR & GAMBLE	4	2
TAMBRANDS	1	2
BOISE CASCADE	4	1
BOWATER	2	2
CHAMPION INTERNATIONAL	3	1
CHESAPEAKE	4	1
CONSOLIDATED PAPERS	3	0
FEDERAL PAPER BOARD	1	3
FORT HOWARD	2	4
GEORGIA-PACIFIC	3	1
GREAT NORTHERN NEKOOSA	4	1
INTERNATIONAL PAPER	3	1

Appendix (Continued)

COMPANY	DIVERSIFICATION	
	RELATED	UNRELATED
JAMES RIVER CO. OF VIRGINIA	6	0
JEFFERSON SMURFIT	1	0
KIMBERLY-CLARK	3	2
LOUISIANA PACIFIC	5	1
MEAD	5	1
POTLATCH	4	1
SCOTT PAPER	4	2
SONOCO	2	3
STONE CONTAINER	1	3
TEMPLE-INLAND	3	3
UNION CAMP	3	2
WESTVACO	6	0
WEYERHAUSER	1	2
WILLAMETTE INDUSTRIES	3	1
CAMERON IRON WORKS	1	2
DRESSER INDUSTRIES	4	2
AMDAHL	1	3
APPLE COMPUTER	1	0
COMPAQ COMPUTER	1	0
DATA GENERAL	1	0
DIGITAL EQUIPMENT	1	1
HEWLETT-PACKARD	3	2
INTERGRAPH	1	1
IBM	3	3
NCR	2	3
PITNEY-BOWES	2	2
PRIME COMPUTER	1	1
SEAGATE TECHNOLOGY	1	0
STANDARD REGISTER	2	1
TANDEM COMPUTERS	1	0
UNISYS	2	2
WANG LABORATORIES	1	1
XEROX	1	4

1987 Ownership Structure Measures Derived from Proxy Statements (in %)

COMPANY	MANAGEMENT STOCKHOLDINGS	STOCK CONCENTRATION
BOEING	1.01	0
LOCKHEED	1.5	0
MARTIN MARIETTA	5.41	0
MCDONNELL DOUGLAS	15.3	0
MAYTAG	1.49	0
WHIRLPOOL	2.9	9.12
CHRYSLER	1.03	0
DANA	0.7	0
ECHLIN	3.43	0
FEDERAL-MOGUL	3.32	28.2
GENERAL MOTORS	0.5	7
MACK TRUCKS	53	22
PACCAR	47.8	36.3
STANDARD PRODUCTS	33.2	28.3
ANHEUSER-BUSCH	13.8	23.3
BROWN-FORMAN	63	7.2
COORS (ADOLPH)	42	21
GENERAL CINEMA	12.03	82.72
PEPSICO	0.4	0
LONE STAR INDUSTRIES	10.98	16.76
MASCO	8.1	5.4
OWENS-CORNING FIBERGLASS	2.7	9.4
SHERWIN-WILLIAMS	1.74	21.15
USG	1.07	9.81
AIR PRODUCTS & CHEMICALS	2.8	0
AMERICAN CYANAMID	1	0
DEXTER	7.8	18
DOW CHEMICAL	1.41	0
ECOLAB	1.7	20.3
ENGLEHARD	52	12
ETHYL	20.57	0
FERRO	2.4	0
FREEPORT-MCMORAN	4.3	18.5
GAF	11.7	17.31
GRACE (W. R.)	6.7	17.8
LUBRIZOL	1	0
MONSANTO	1	0
MORTON THIOKOL	1.6	5
NALCO CHEMICAL	1.8	7.49
OLIN	5	0
PENNWALT	1.3	16.3
ROHM & HAAS	49.2	32.4
UNION CARBIDE	0.4	5.7
WITCO	5.2	24.7
ALLIED-SIGNAL	0.4	7.5

Appendix (Continued)

COMPANY	MANAGEMENT STOCKHOLDINGS	STOCK CONCENTRATION
FIGGIE INTERNATIONAL	64	25
IC INDUSTRIES	1.47	0
ITT	1	0
ROCKWELL INTERNATIONAL	1	0
TELEDYNE	27.8	0
TENNECO	1	0
BALL	5.15	0
ABBOTT LABS	0.2	6.2
AMERICAN HOME PRODUCTS	0.6	0
BARD (C. R.)	2.08	0
BAXTER TRAVENOL LABS	2.2	0
BECTON DICKINSON	2.5	7.7
BRISTOL-MEYERS	2.09	0
JOHNSON & JOHNSON	1.5	8.4
LILLY (ELI)	0.41	17.98
MARION LABS	24.5	0
MERCK	1	0
PFIZER	1	0
SCHERING-PLOUGH	0.5	0
SMITHKLINE BECKMAN	1.11	0
SQUIBB	1.8	0
UPJOHN	4.8	0
WARNER-LAMBERT	0.7	0
AMETEK	5	0
AMP	1.34	0
CHAMPION SPARK PLUG	4.29	86
COMBUSTION ENGINEERING	1.2	16
GENERAL INSTRUMENT	1.8	0
HARRIS	1.7	0
LITTON INDUSTRIES	4.28	27.62
MEDTRONIC	4.39	8.73
AMERICAN BRANDS	1	0
PHILIP MORRIS	0.49	0
UST	5.8	0
COOPER TIRE & RUBBER	5	28.8
GOODYEAR TIRE & RUBBER	0.9	0
MOTOROLA	6.5	6.2
RAYTHEON	1	0
SQUARE D	1.97	7.78
TRW	1	0
TEXAS INSTRUMENT	1.6	10.3
WESTINGHOUSE ELECTRIC	1	0
ARCHER DANIELS MIDLAND	13.5	6.3
BORDEN	0.57	0
CAMPBELL SOUP	8.1	57.7
CPC INTERNATIONAL	1	7.54

Appendix (Continued)

COMPANY	MANAGEMENT STOCKHOLDINGS	STOCK CONCENTRATION
CONAGRA	9.9	0
DEAN FOODS	3.4	5.6
GENERAL MILLS	1.75	0
GERBER PRODUCTS	7.66	11.4
HEINZ (H. J.)	11.73	39.59
HERSHEY FOODS	0.3	30.6
HORMEL (GEO. A.)	1.59	50.72
INTERNATIONAL MULTIFOODS	3.98	30.32
KELLOGG	1	84.16
KRAFT	0.9	0
MCCORMICK	59	40
QUAKER OATS	2.13	0
RALSTON PURINA	6.31	14.8
SARA LEE	1.89	0
TYSON FOODS	57	39
UNIVERSAL FOODS	13.8	9.4
WRIGLEY (WM. JR.)	36.48	54.57
CINCINNATI MILICRON	9.25	29.95
INGERSOLL-RAND	1	5.1
INTERLAKE	4.6	24.3
SUNDSTRAND	1.6	0
FOXBORO	24.3	37.4
JOHNSON CONTROLS	1.8	11.5
PERKIN ELMER	1	0
TEKTRONIX	12.52	35.7
AMERICAN GREETINGS	47	28
BRUNSWICK	4.1	0
EASTMAN KODAK	1	0
FLEETWOOD ENTERPRISES	21.2	18.3
HASBRO	28.1	40.01
MATTEL	23	32.7
OUTBOARD MARINE	1.58	28.62
POALROID	1	7.7
ALCOA	1	5.3
NEWMONT MINING	0.3	49.35
BASSETT FURNITURE INDUSTRIES	60	32
BEMIS	11	12.3
BLACK & DECKER	1	0
HARTMARX	1.6	14.2
INTERCO	1.14	9.29
SHAW INDUSTRIES	16.9	29.9
SPRING INDUSTRIES	1.89	57.75
VF	17.3	6.6
WORTHINGTON INDUSTRIES	64	34
COOPER INDUSTRIES	1	0
DOVER	10.87	0

Appendix (Continued)

COMPANY	MANAGEMENT STOCKHOLDINGS	STOCK CONCENTRATION
FMC	3.9	29.8
DELUXE CHECK PRINTERS	0.5	0
DONNELLY (R. R.) & SONS	5.3	9.4
COMMERCE CLEARING HOUSE	59	36
DOW JONES	25.3	29
GANNETT	1.4	0
HARCOURT BRACE JOVANOVICH	6.3	48.7
KNIGHT-RIDDER	41.26	14.4
MACMILLAN	5.5	0
MEDIA GENERAL	13.4	37.7
MEREDITH	13	7.3
NEW YORK TIMES	61	38
TIME, INC.	10.6	6.9
TIMES MIRROR	34.71	0
TRIBUNE CO.	22	16.8
WASHINGTON POST	81.1	0
CORNING GLASS WORKS	4.44	15.6
CRANE	1.7	10.4
AMOCO	1	5.8
ASHLAND OIL	1.5	28.7
CHEVRON	0.1	0
EXXON	0.1	0
KERR-MCGEE	4.47	0
MAPCO	4.8	18.05
MOBIL	1.2	6
MURPHEY OIL	23.3	7.9
NERCO	1	89.9
SUN	1	26.4
TEXACO	1	14.8
UNOCAL	1	7.4
AVON PRODUCTS	3.3	13.5
COLGATE-PALMOLIVE	1.83	26.52
GILLETTE	1.3	0
INT'L FLAVORS & FRAGRANCES	19.2	19.9
PROCTOR & GAMBLE	0.83	5.59
TAMBRANDS	1.96	5.05
BOISE CASCADE	3.1	5.15
BOWATER	1	17.21
CHAMPION INTERNATIONAL	1	0
CHESAPEAKE	18.2	22.2
CONSOLIDATED PAPERS	60	37
FEDERAL PAPER BOARD	7.1	25.69
FORT HOWARD	1.5	79
GEORGIA-PACIFIC	2.1	0
GREAT NORTHERN NEKOOSA	0.7	0
INTERNATIONAL PAPER	0.6	8.43

Appendix (Continued)

COMPANY	MANAGEMENT STOCKHOLDINGS	STOCK CONCENTRATION
JAMES RIVER CO. OF VIRGINIA	2	7.7
JEFFERSON SMURFIT	51	34
KIMBERLY-CLARK	1	5.5
LOUISIANA PACIFIC	1.5	0
MEAD	3.4	5.1
POTLATCH	13.4	5.7
SCOTT PAPER	1.2	5.35
SONOCO	54	31
STONE CONTAINER	18.5	5.2
TEMPLE-INLAND	2.7	0
UNION CAMP	1	0
WESTVACO	1.5	0
WEYERHAUSER	6.9	0
WILLAMETTE INDUSTRIES	57	36
CAMERON IRON WORKS	9.5	31.73
DRESSER INDUSTRIES	1	6.22
AMDAHL	1.45	44.74
APPLE COMPUTER	48	5
COMPAQ COMPUTER	5.15	0
DATA GENERAL	11.9	21.8
DIGITAL EQUIPMENT	3.8	0
HEWLETT-PACKARD	29.1	0
INTERGRAPH	54	20
IBM	0.5	0
NCR	1.7	0
PITNEY-BOWES	1	14.9
PRIME COMPUTER	0.9	11.4
SEAGATE TECHNOLOGY	57	10
STANDARD REGISTER	58	15
TANDEM COMPUTERS	4.7	0
UNISYS	0.7	0
WANG LABORATORIES	38.4	43.1
XEROX	0.01	0

6

DETERMINANTS OF CEO COMPENSATION: AN ASSESSMENT AND GUIDE

THE EXECUTIVE COMPENSATION VALUATION MODEL

In Chapter 5 we tested an executive compensation valuation model based on a regression model linking executive compensation to financial performance, size, diversification strategy, and ownership structure, measured by both stock concentration and management stockholdings. The two ownership structure variables were introduced either directly, in a strictly linear model, or with turning points of 5 and 25 percent, in a nonmonotonic model. The results overwhelmingly show that a nonmonotonic formulation is not an appropriate model for executive compensation. The best executive compensation valuation model was obtained with a strictly linear model linking the log of compensation divided by total assets to related diversification, unrelated diversification, management stockholdings, stock concentration, and financial performance, measured as the logarithm of market value over total assets. While the above results are indicative of the potential of a linear regression-based executive compensation valuation model, they fail to reflect the richer environment that can be provided by the direct and indirect effects of all the variables cited. To that effect we judged the linear regression model from Table 5.6 adequate but not sufficient for a complete understanding of the determinants of executive compensation in the United States. The next sections will, therefore, concentrate on assessing the path model results.

THE EXECUTIVE COMPENSATION PATH MODEL

The results of the path model as reported in Chapter 5 show the importance of size, management stockholdings, stock concentration, related diversification, unrelated diversification, and firm performance on executive compensation, as well as the presence of interesting direct and indirect effects, reflecting a richer environment than portrayed by a linear regression valuation model. In what follows the implications of the direct and indirect effects are discussed.

DIRECT EFFECTS

Ownership Structure and Executive Compensation

We hypothesized that the interests of owners and managers differ. In owner-controlled firms, owners have an important say in the level and structure of executive compensation and may find themselves in direct competition with the managers for the appropriate distribution of the total return of the firm. Our expectation was that they would prefer to vote a higher share of the return to themselves, implying a negative relationship between stock concentration and executive compensation. The direct effect of stock concentration was indeed found to be negative. This lends support to the generally held view that powerful stockholders may vote a higher share of the resources to themselves rather than to the executives. This also added to the established result that owner-controlled firms replace executives more frequently. When performance declines, the news does not bid well for managers in owner-controlled firms.

We also hypothesized that the managers in manager-controlled firms are more likely to view factors other than performance as the basis of their pay. In addition, given that they hold enough voting power to guarantee their jobs, they may favor pay packages that include bonuses and long-term income as opposed to base salary. Our expectation was that they would prefer other rewards than base salary, implying a negative relationship between management stockholdings and executive compensation. The direct effect of management stockholdings was indeed found to be negative. It lends support to the view that powerful managers may prefer pay packages favoring bonuses and long-term income rather than base salary.

Ownership Structure and Firm Performance

The empirical relationship between performance and corporate ownership structure is characterized by mixed results supporting both the convergence-of-interests hypothesis and the entrenchment hypothesis. While we agree with these two theoretical rationales, we believe that they apply differently.

The understanding under the management stockholdings thesis is as follows. With low management stockholdings and low and diffused stock ownership, managers may use corporate assets to benefit themselves rather than their shareholders. With increased management stockholdings, managers are less tempted to squander corporate wealth and more interested in increasing firm returns in accordance with the convergence-of-interests hypothesis. However, with increased management stockholdings beyond certain critical levels, managers hold enough power to forego value-maximization behavior in conformity with the

at Stockholdings and Firm Performance

PEk.. RMANCE

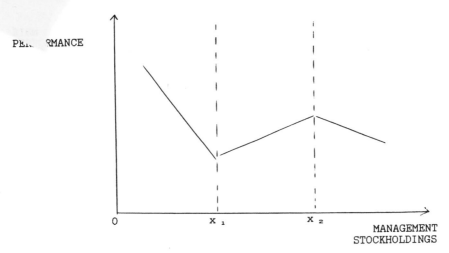

0   X $_1$ X $_2$

MANAGEMENT
STOCKHOLDINGS

entrenchment hypothesis. What all this discussion implies is that the relationship between management stockholdings and performance will be negative for low levels of management stockholdings up to a point, where it will become positive to revert at a higher point to a negative relationship (see Figure 6.1). Our expectation was that, given the high ranges of management stockholdings among firms in the Fortune 500, the relationship between management stockholdings and financial performance would be negative. However, our findings of a positive relationship between management stockholdings and firm performance indicates that the managers did not own enough voting power to focus on nonvalue-maximization behavior as indicated by the entrenchment hypothesis. On the contrary, managers in our sample owned a sufficient share of the firms to justify a convergence of interests with the shareholders on return maximization.

The understanding under the stock concentration thesis is as follows. With low stockholdings and diffuse stock ownership, stockholders are not in a position to insure effective wealth maximization and cooperation from managers. Therefore with low levels of stockholdings, in accordance with the convergence-of-interest hypothesis, decreasing firm returns may occur. With a large concentration of ownership, however, the stockholders can dictate terms to insure wealth maximization of managers, resulting in increasing firm returns (see Figure 6.2). Our expectation was that, given the high ranges of stock concentration among firms in the Fortune 500, the relationship between stock concentration and firm performance would be positive. The findings, however, were that, in fact, the low levels of stock concentration in our sample did not allow

Figure 6.2
Stock Concentration and Firm Performance

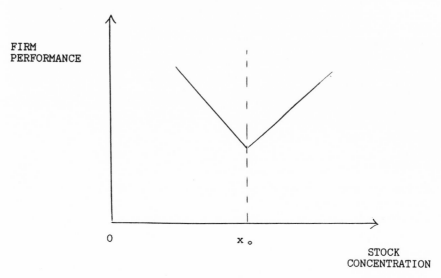

the stockholders to overcome the information asymmetries and force management to act in the stockholders' interest.

Diversification Strategy and Firm Performance

Following theoretical constructs based on the combined effect of the implementation of the m-form and different diversification strategies, our expectation was that the firm performance would be positively related to related diversification and negatively related to unrelated diversification. The negative relationships between the two types of diversification strategy and firm performance are consistent with the theory and other studies, in the case of unrelated diversification, and different, in the case of related diversification. The evidence we found indicated that related diversification is not associated with superior economic reteurn. The same phenomenon has been observed in other recent studies with the rationale that the decline in performance may be due to the lack of ability to allocate resources among interdependent divisions.

Diversification Strategy
and Executive Compensation

Our thesis maintains that compensation practices may drive diversification strategies. Another thesis maintains that executive compensation is a potential form of discretionary behavior, and that under a decentralized structure, it would be better controlled. Our expectation is that whatever the diversification strategies adopted, the control arrangements necessary to implement the decentralization are complex and costly, and justify higher executive compensation. Therefore, a positive relationship between executive compensation and either diversification strategy is assumed. Our findings of a positive relationship between the two types of diversification strategies and executive compensation are consistent with the view that control arrangements under the m-form of organization are more demanding than under the u-form, dictating the need for higher pay for executives in companies adopting either a related or unrelated diversification strategy.

Effects of Size

Our expectation was that firm size would be: (1) positively related to both diversification strategies, related and unrelated, given that both strategies imply a growing and expanding firm; (2) positively related to firm performance given that bigger firms may have more resources to devote to profitable opportunities; and (3) positively related to compensation given that bigger firms tend to pay more to executives who are overseeing substantial resources, and also have the ability to do so. The empirical results verified all three expectations about the positive effects of firm size.

INDIRECT EFFECTS

The central thesis and attraction in using a path model is the determination of interesting indirect effects in addition to direct effects. Accordingly, our most important results confirm that, in addition to direct effects, size, ownership structure, and diversification strategy have an indirect effect on executive compensation through the impact and/or influence of firm performance. These mediating relationships support the contentions that: (1) economic performance can be used as a key justification by owners and managers in the final determination of executive compensation; and (2) firm size, ownership structure, and the extent of related and unrelated diversification can be used as determinants of executive compensation when associated with the right economic performance.

The first mediating relationship is in line with earlier research studies confirming the positive and important relationship between executive compensation and financial performance. Ceteris paribus the better the financial peformance of the firm the higher the executive compensation. As it should be, firm performance is used to monitor the executive's performance and the reward system. While this result may appear to be a sound management relationship, it points to the potential motivations of executives to adopt strategies, pursue projects, and even manage profit in a manner that ensures a short-term profit maximization. One bit of advice at this level is to tie executive compensation to long-term performance and long-term operating income, which may be less susceptible to manipulation through widely known income-smoothing techniques.

The second mediating relationship points to an interesting phenomenon concerning the indirect impact of size, ownership structure, and related and unrelated diversification. This impact on and importance to the compensation level and structure goes in tandem with a positive economic performance. In other words, the factors of size, ownership structure, and related and unrelated diversification strategy are salient factors only when they are linked to or in the presence of a strong financial performance.

To recapitulate, here are the most important findings in examining the impact of the determinants of the level of CEO compensation among a sample of Fortune 500 firms:

1. Approximately 75 percent of the effect of stock concentration was direct and 25 percent was mediated by firm performance and management stockholdings.
2. Approximately 70 percent of the effect of management stockholdings was direct and 30 percent was mediated by firm performance.
3. Approximately 80 percent of the effect of related diversification was direct and 20 percent was mediated by firm performance.
4. Approximately 75 percent of the effect of unrelated diversification was direct and 25 percent was mediated by firm performance.
5. Approximately 85 percent of the effect of size was direct and 15 percent was mediated by firm performance.

Those interested in understanding the levels of executive compensation among Fortune 500 firms are advised to view the relationship of the determinants of executive compensation to be not only direct, as generally assumed in most valuation models, but also indirect, as assumed by our path model. This chapter has explained the nature and the ramifications of both the direct and indirect effects, and has offered specific scoring rules for ascertaining the mediating effects of size, ownership structure, and diversification strategy on executive compensation. These rules should be a good anchor for an understanding of the complexity and level of managerial compensation, and a good guide to an assessment of the adequacy of managerial compensation in any complete financial analysis of a firm's potential.

INDEX

About the Authors

ELLEN L. PAVLIK is Assistant Professor of Accounting at Loyola University of Chicago.

AHMED BELKAOUI is Professor of Accounting at the University of Illinois at Chicago and the author of more than 20 accounting texts and monographs.